DESERTED
NEW ORLEANS

A JOURNEY THROUGH ABANDONED LANDMARKS

NOLADEEJ

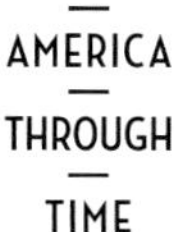

Aᴍᴇʀɪᴄᴀ Tʜʀᴏᴜɢʜ Tɪᴍᴇ®
An imprint of Sᴜᴛᴛᴏɴ Pᴜʙʟɪsʜɪɴɢ Iɴᴄ.
www.through-time.com

First published 2025
Copyright © NOLADEEJ 2025

ISBN 978-1-63499-540-5

Typeset in Trade Gothic 10pt on 15pt
Printed and bound in England

CONTENTS

INTRODUCTION

Growing up in the New Orleans area, you experience a city that feels like nowhere else. New Orleans is not just one city; it is an entire metropolitan area with neighboring communities like Metairie, Kenner, Gretna, Algiers, LaPlace, Arabi, Chalmette, and many more. Together, they create a tapestry of neighborhoods, people, and stories that contribute to the shared culture of this place.

Within New Orleans itself, neighborhoods like the French Quarter, the Garden District, Treme, and the Lower Ninth Ward have become iconic for their culture, history, and architecture. Each has its own lively energy and deep heritage. Unfortunately, there are also parts of the city that have been lost. Places that once thrived now stand deserted and left to Mother Nature, vandalism, squatters, and the curiosity of urban explorers.

I am one of those explorers. For as long as I can remember, I have been drawn to old, deserted places. My love for history and my sense of adventure led me to these sites, where I document and photograph what remains, hoping to preserve a glimpse of these places before they are lost forever. A few years ago, I teamed up with several other fellow explorers and together we formed a group we named Krewe du Exploration, similar to a Mardi Gras organization using the word "krewe" for their group.

In this book, I invite you to join me and the krewe on a journey to uncover hidden corners in and around New Orleans. You may notice that quite a few, but not all, of these locations were greatly affected by Hurricane Katrina in 2005. Some locations may be familiar, while others might reveal a side of the city you have never seen. From the deserted Six Flags theme park to a power plant on the Mississippi River, a towering skyscraper, a huge naval base, a Civil Defense fallout shelter deep underground, and an apartment complex turned art installation, each site has its own story to tell.

We explore places like a prominent Catholic high school, an orphanage with a dark past, a hospital that witnessed tragedy during Hurricane Katrina, an iconic newspaper plant, and a nursing home with an unusual history. Each of these places holds a unique layer of history, and through my eyes and lens, I hope to share their stories with you.

Author's Note

This book is the result of years of exploration, photography, and research into the abandoned spaces of New Orleans and its surrounding areas. While the photos and experiences are my own, much of the historical context was gathered through a combination of news archives, public records, preservation reports, and other publicly available resources.

I am not a historian. My goal is not to give a definitive account of each location's past but to share what I have learned and experienced while documenting these places before they disappear completely.

Whenever possible, I cross-referenced multiple sources to ensure accuracy, but given the nature of some of these sites, details may vary or remain incomplete.

Sources used for information in this book include:
-        The Times-Picayune / NOLA.com Archives
-        Preservation Resource Center of New Orleans
-        The Historic New Orleans Collection
-        Coasterpedia.net
-        New Orleans Historical (neworleanshistorical.org)
-        Holy Cross School Website
-        Abandoned Southeast (abandonedsoutheast.com)
-        Alchetron.com
-        Nolaghosts.com
-        Wikipedia (cross-checked with other sources)

1

JAZZLAND/SIX FLAGS NEW ORLEANS

From Thrills to Silence in the Shadow of Katrina

In the heart of New Orleans East, nestled in the shadow of the vast marshlands, lies a haunting relic of a time when laughter, thrill, and joy filled the air. Six Flags New Orleans, originally known as Jazzland, is a place frozen in time, slowly being reclaimed by nature.

According to Coasterpedia.net, the idea of Jazzland began in the late 1990s and was envisioned as a vibrant amusement park that would celebrate the spirit of New Orleans. Opening its gates in the year 2000, Jazzland was designed to offer both locals and tourists a world of fun and excitement. With several themed areas, each reflecting a different aspect of New Orleans and Louisiana culture, Jazzland aimed to capture the essence of the region.

Despite its ambitious vision, the park struggled to attract the expected crowds. Financial troubles plagued it from the start, and after just two seasons, it filed for bankruptcy. However, in 2002, Six Flags, the national amusement park chain, acquired the struggling park, hoping to breathe new life into it.

Under new ownership, it was rebranded and in 2003 reopened as Six Flags New Orleans. The company invested in new attractions and introduced popular new roller coasters like Batman: The Ride. It kept most of the original attractions including the Mega Zeph, a wooden coaster that paid homage to the Zephyr, a popular roller coaster from New Orleans' old Pontchartrain Beach Amusement Park.

On August 29, 2005, Hurricane Katrina made landfall in Louisiana, bringing with it catastrophic winds and storm surges. The park was inundated with floodwaters that remained for weeks, causing major damage to the rides, buildings, and infrastructure.

The devastation was so complete that Six Flags quickly determined the park was beyond repair. The company announced that it would not reopen the park and abandoned it, though a few of the rides would be relocated to other parks.

Photographers and filmmakers have been drawn to the site, capturing the haunting beauty of the decaying park. It has served as a backdrop for movies, music videos, and countless photographs and videos.

The Krewe du Exploration chose to enter the park just before sunrise so we could be as inconspicuous as possible. A brief overnight rain had left the ground damp, with the lingering scent of rain adding to the park's haunting ambiance. We had heard of encounters with alligators, wild boar, and snakes, but that did not deter us from this adventure.

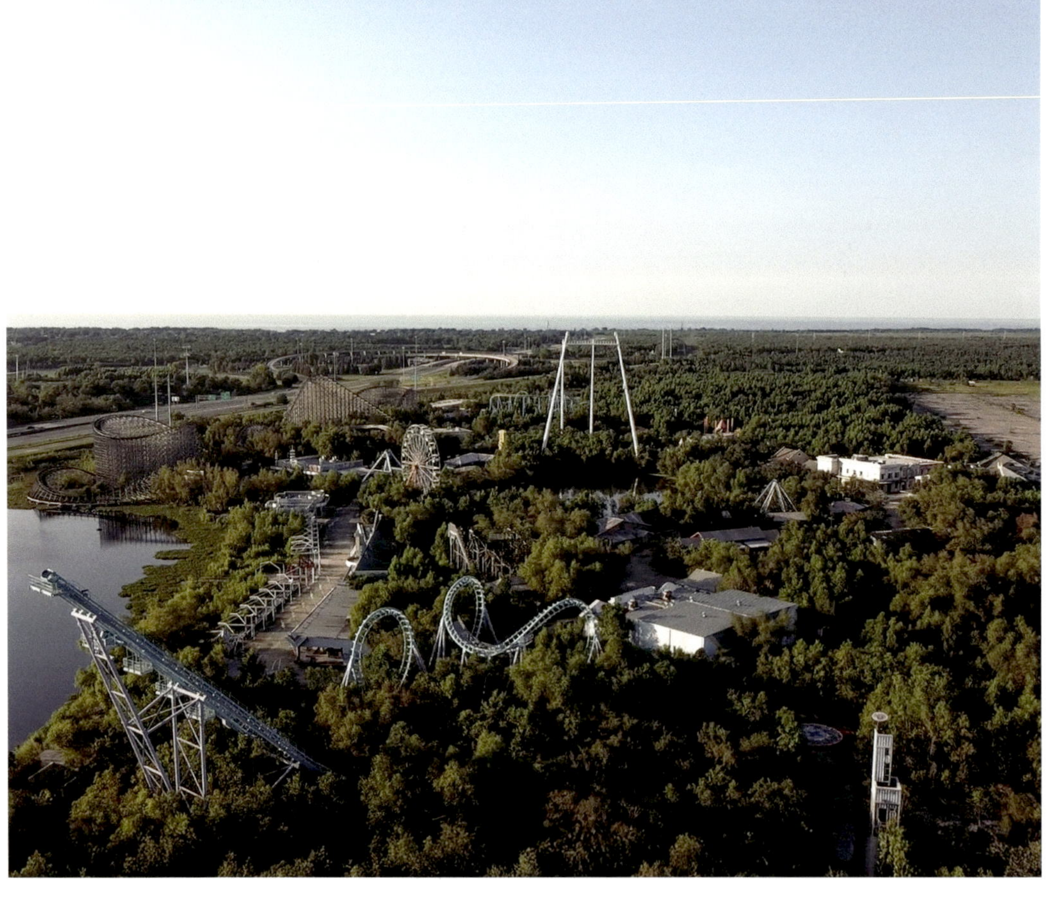

An aerial view of the deserted Six Flags New Orleans, once a lively theme park filled with families and laughter. Opened in 2000 as Jazzland, it was later rebranded as Six Flags in 2003. The park thrived briefly before being forced to close in 2005 due to the devastating impact of Hurricane Katrina.

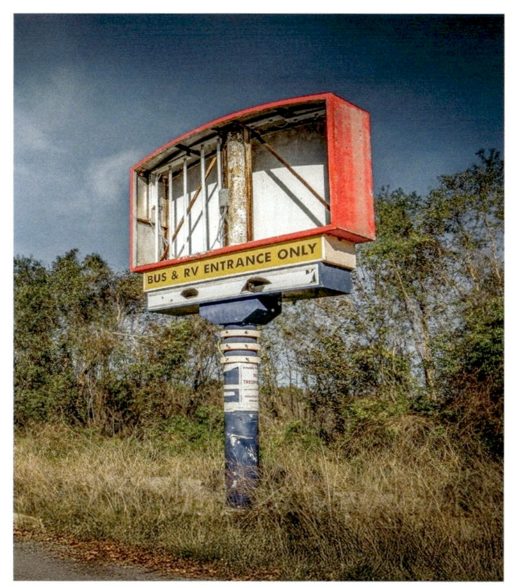
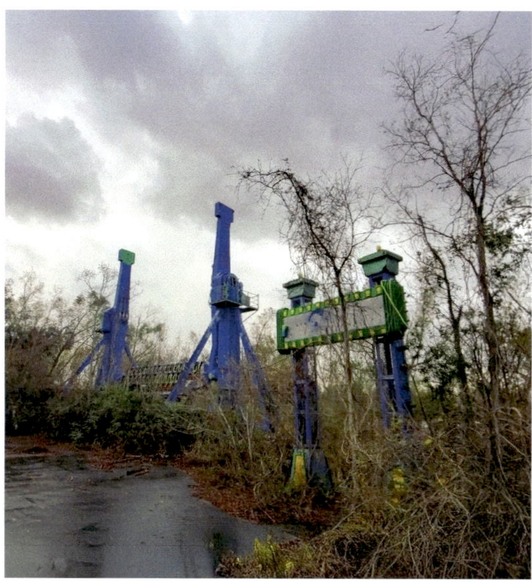

Above left: The weathered sign at the entrance that once read "Closed for Storm" now sits empty and broken. Nearly two decades later, the park remains sealed off, with warning signs trying to keep out those drawn to its decaying beauty.

Above right: Lex Luthor's Invertatron ride stands frozen in time. A rusting skeleton surrounded by tangled vines and cracked asphalt. The battered sign still clinging to its faded colors, as if trying to recall the joy it once promised.

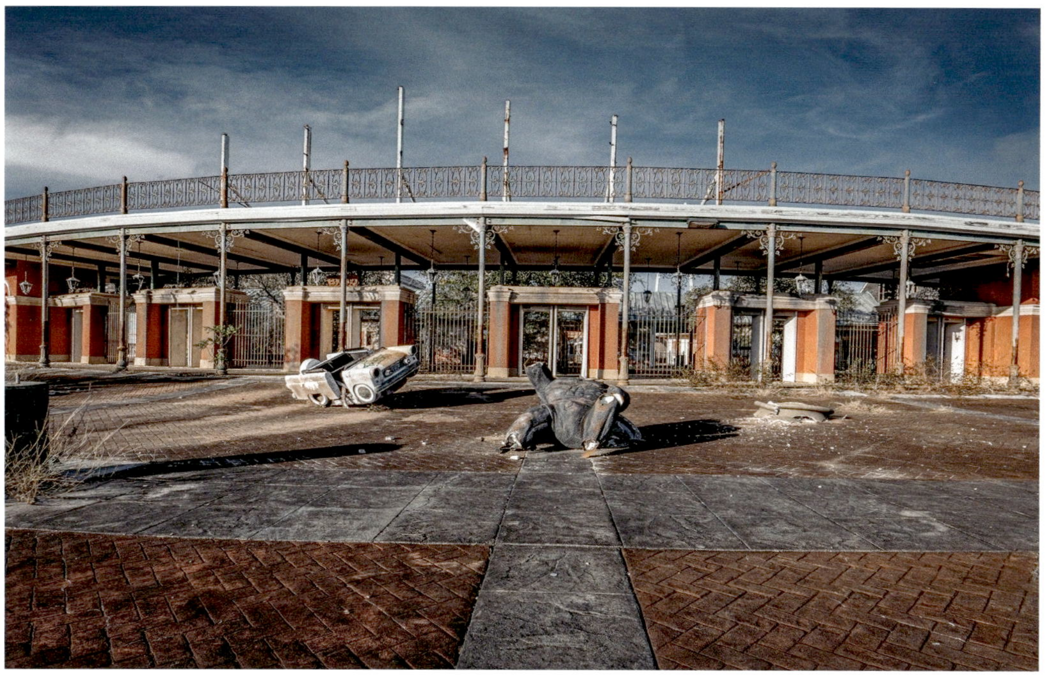

The entrance plaza stands deserted, its pathways overtaken by weeds and cracked concrete. A rusting car from Joker's Jukebox and remnants of a plastic statue now mark the lifeless scene where crowds entered the park.

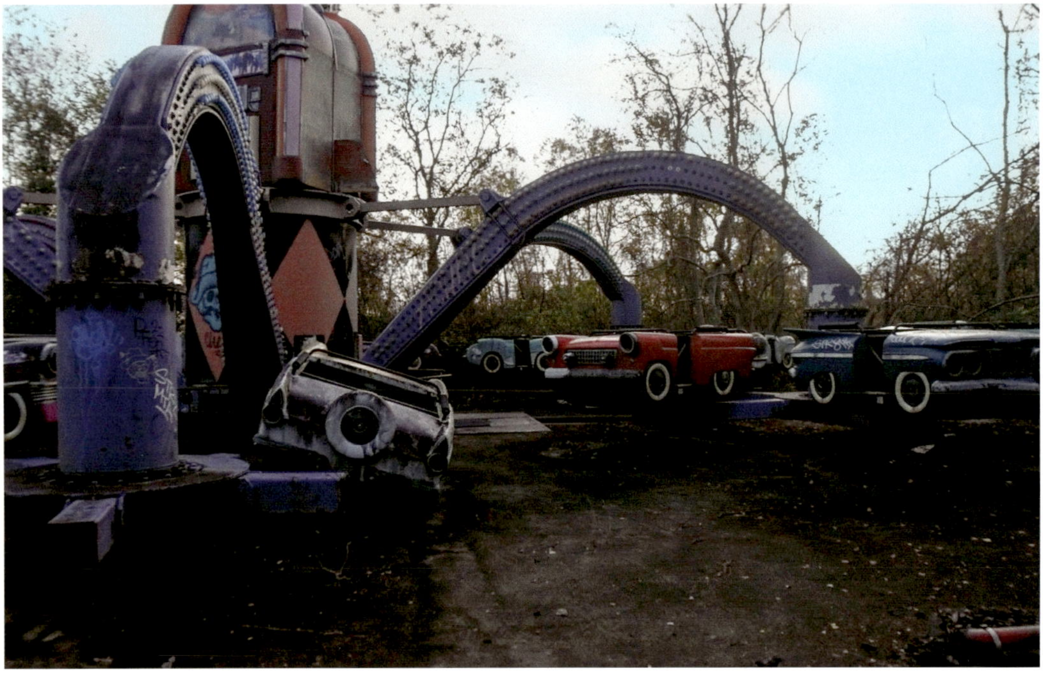

Joker's Jukebox, a spinning ride added when Six Flags took over the park. The classic car ride sits frozen and rusting, its vibrant colors fading under years of neglect. The cheerful cars now coated in graffiti and weathered by time.

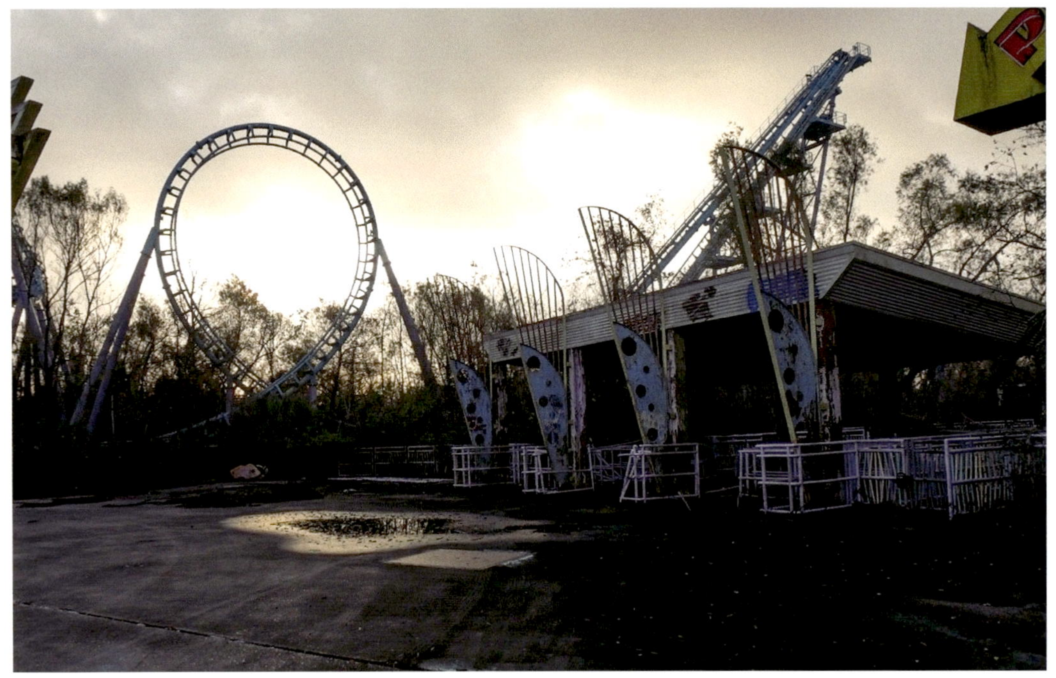

The queue for the Pontchartrain Flyer ride now stands empty. In the background, the Zydeco Scream roller coaster looming silently against the setting sun, its tracks rusted and forgotten.

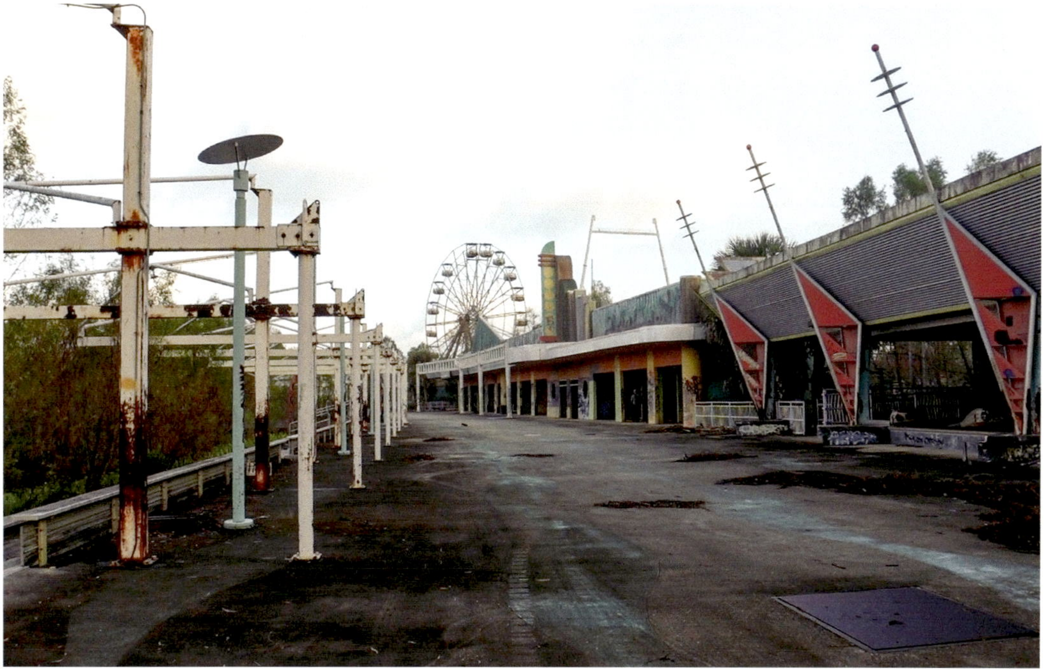

Looking down what once was the Pontchartrain Beach walkway, we see an area for water shows and paddle boats to the left, while the Beach Bang-Up Bumper Cars and the distant Big Easy Ferris Wheel sit to the right.

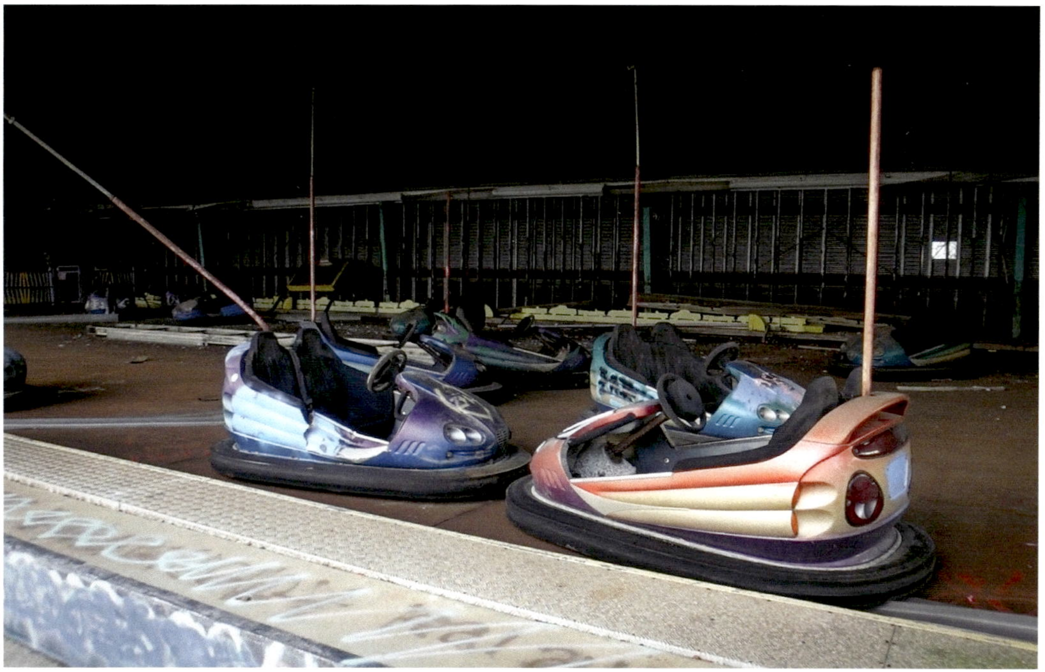

The bumper cars sit lifeless, gathering dust and cobwebs in their old arena. Graffiti and dirt cover the walls where excited screams and laughter used to echo. The once-colorful ride has lost its shine, left to decay in the shadows of the old park.

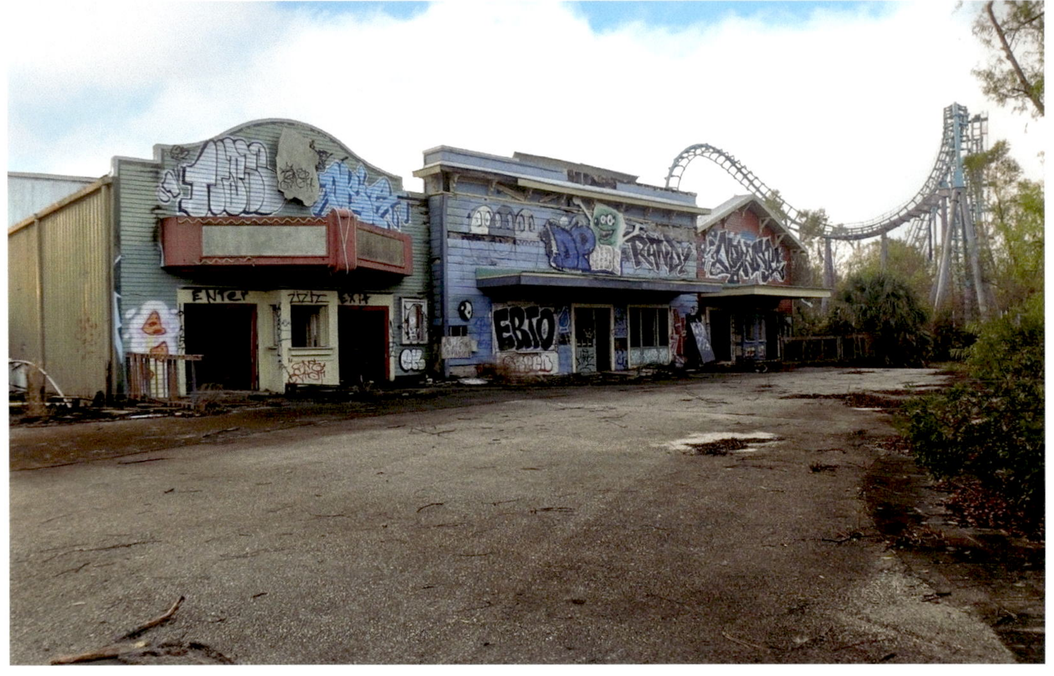

These buildings once housed a 4D pirate adventure before changing to the Spongebob Squarepants Ride. It was a motion simulator with a projector screen and moving seats, but it is now just a shell of what it used to be.

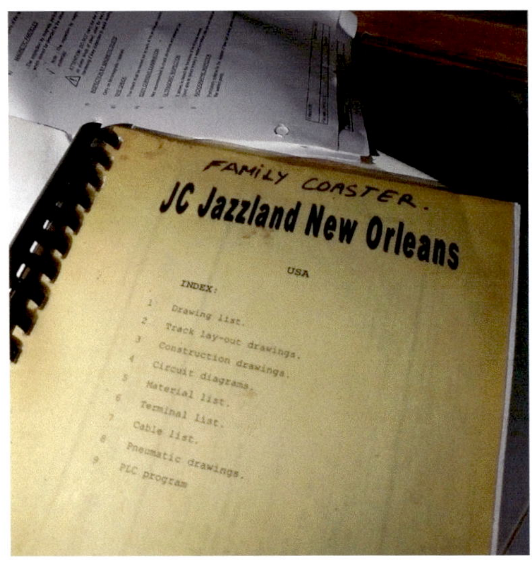

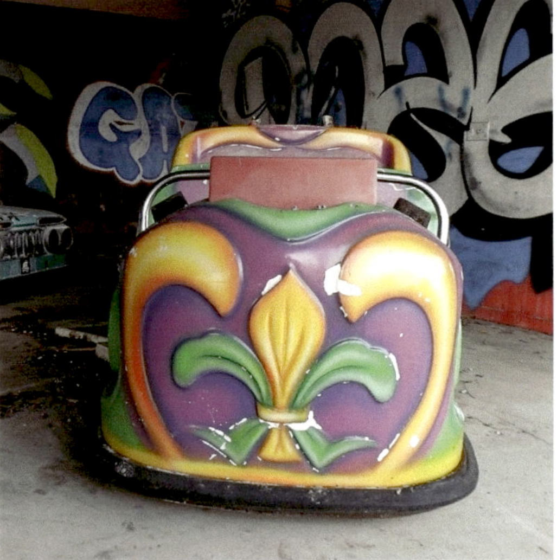

Above left: Hidden among the debris of an office, this dusty manual for the Family Coaster at Jazzland prior to the Six Flags takeover offers a glimpse into the park's past operations. Plans and layouts that are now forgotten relics, left to rot away alongside the rides they once guided.

Above right: A fleur-de-lis-themed car from Jocco's Mardi Gras Madness sits far from its respective ride. Over the years, various people have relocated pieces of rides and structures around the park for their amusement.

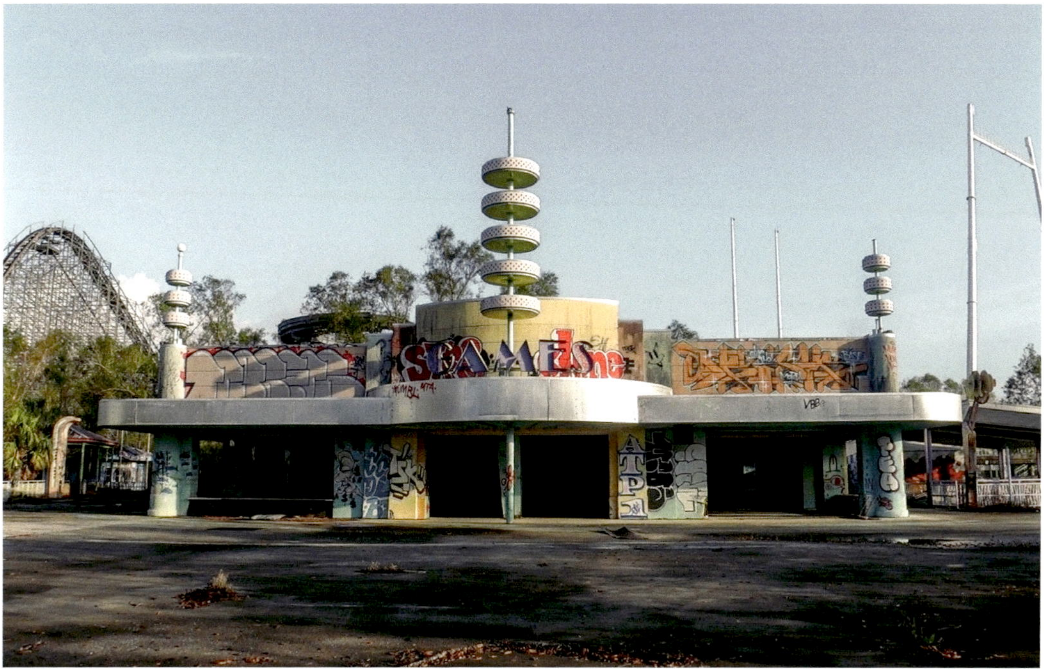

The arcade was a unique building that once buzzed with the latest sounds and screens of video games. It now sits empty and quiet.

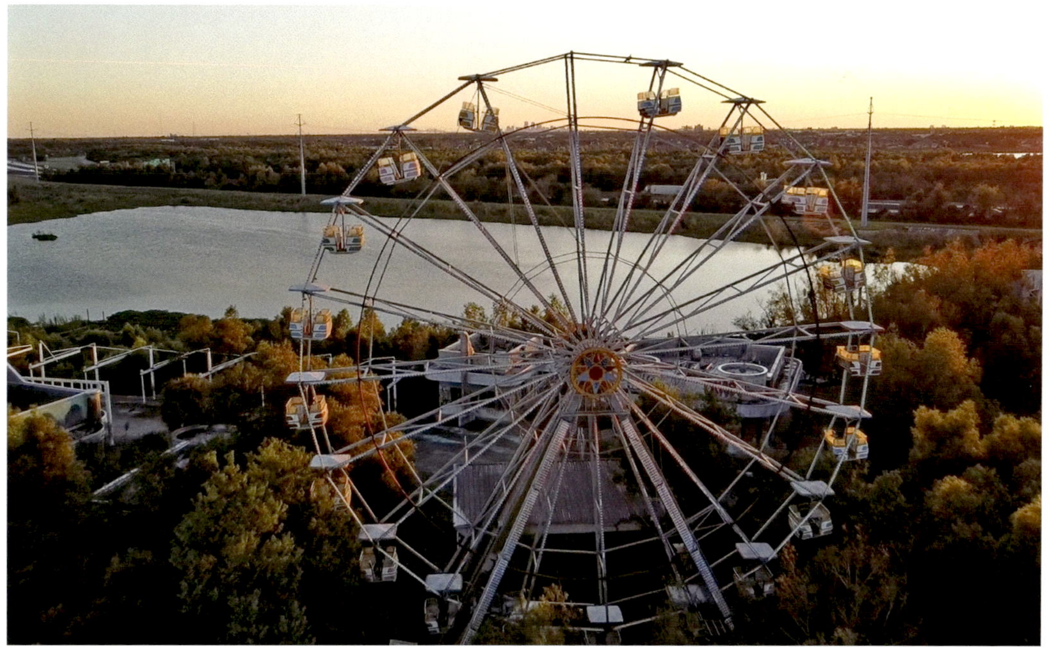

As the sun begins to set, the Big Easy Ferris Wheel casts long shadows on the overgrown park. You will notice that one of its gondolas is missing. It was removed, with permission, to be used for an art installation at Joe W. Brown Memorial Park.

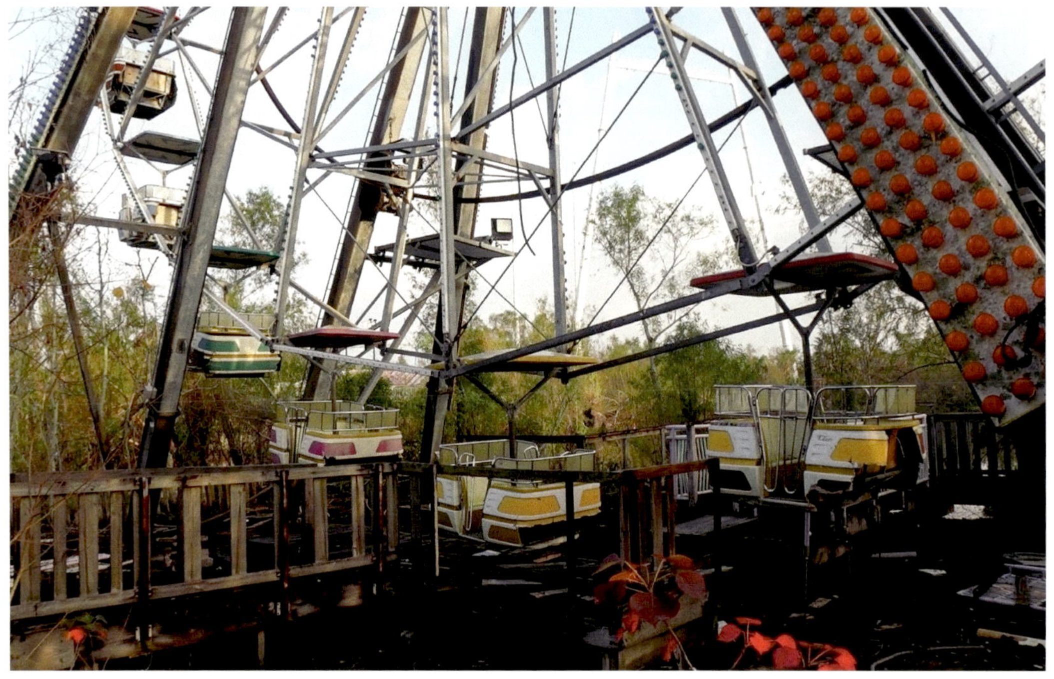

Up close, the Ferris wheel reveals its true state of decay. The faded seats are rusted and broken. The wooden walkway is rotting away, a reminder of how quickly nature reclaims what is left behind. As the wind picks up, the creaking of each of the gondolas swaying on the Ferris wheel make for a haunting sound.

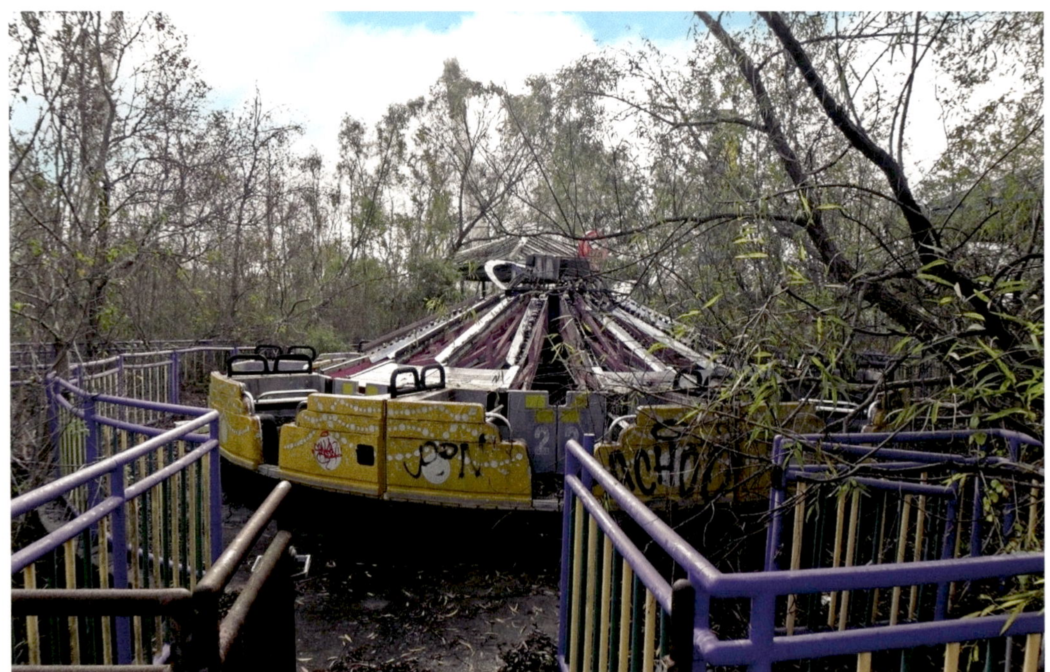

Tucked away behind overgrown branches and rusting gates, the Mad Rex ride is locked in a state of creepy stillness. The bright colors have faded, taken over by weeds with each seat covered in dust and cobwebs.

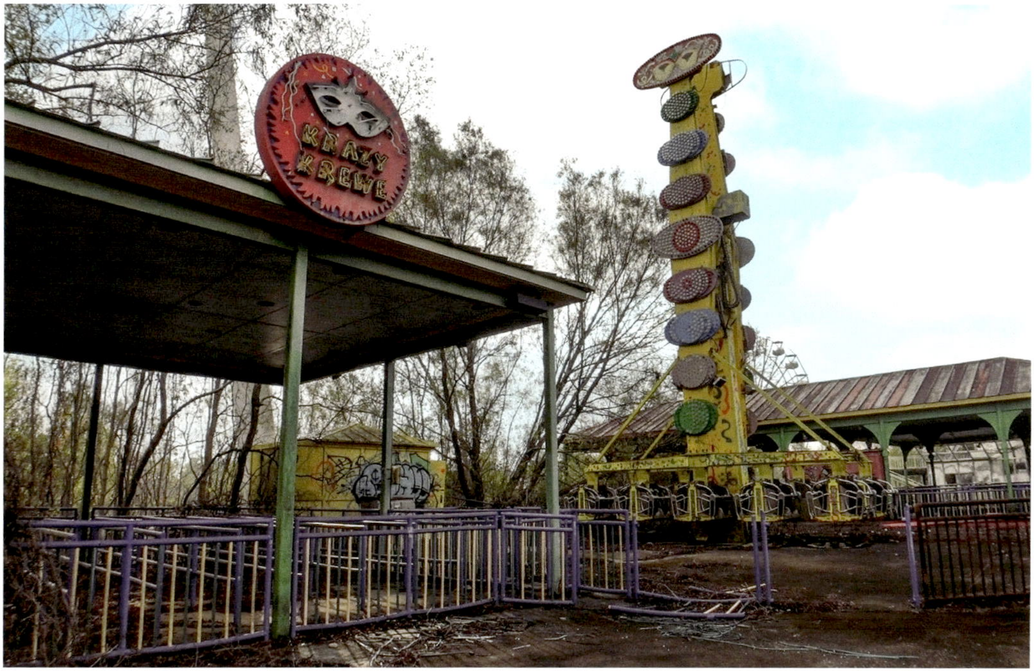

The Krazy Krewe, a thrilling pendulum ride, now hangs in silence and is surrounded by an empty queue and overgrown foliage. The laughter and screams of thrill-seekers have been replaced by the rustle of wind through the trees and creaking metal.

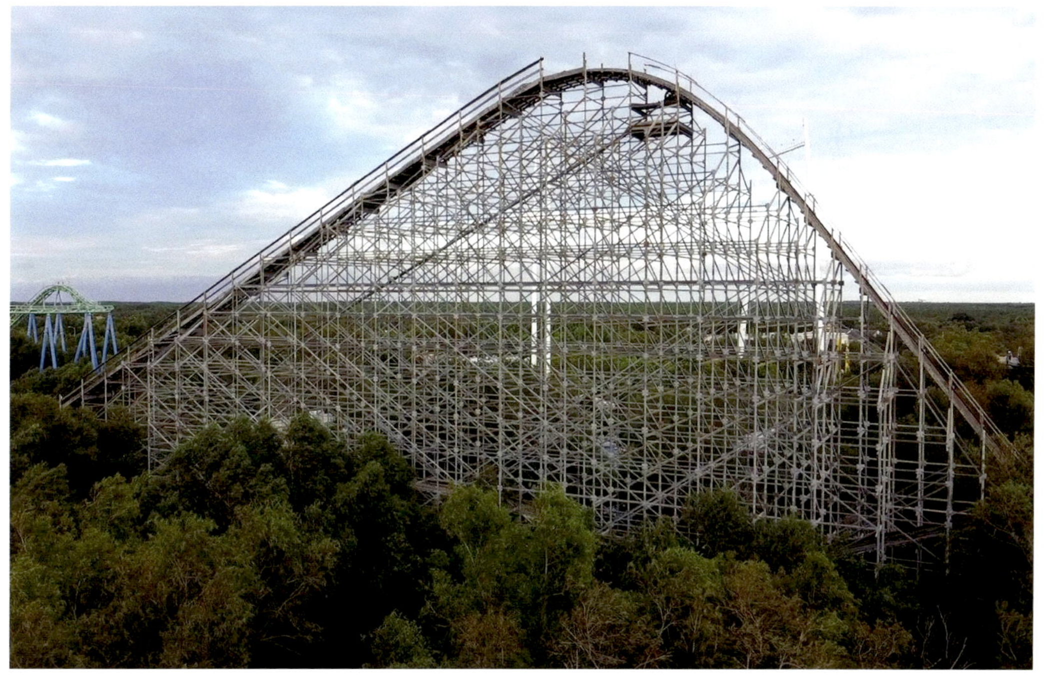

The Mega Zeph wooden roller coaster was built to pay homage to the legendary Zephyr coaster from the old Pontchartrain Beach Amusement Park which closed in 1983. Its tracks, along with The Jester's tracks in the distance, still rise proudly above the trees, a skeletal giant standing against the sky as it attempts to survive the years.

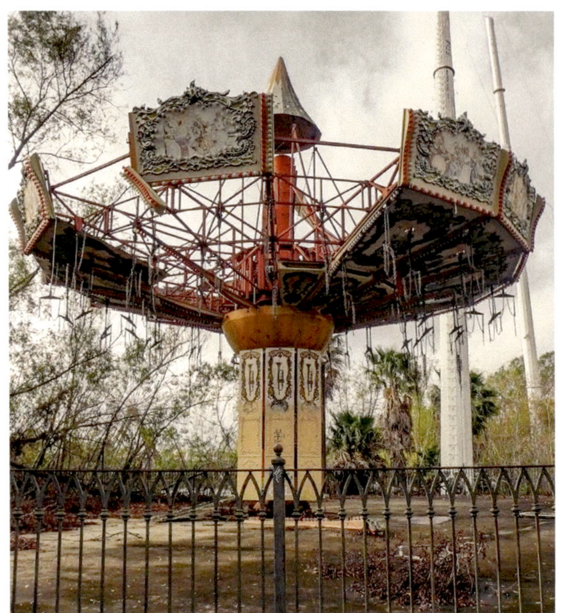

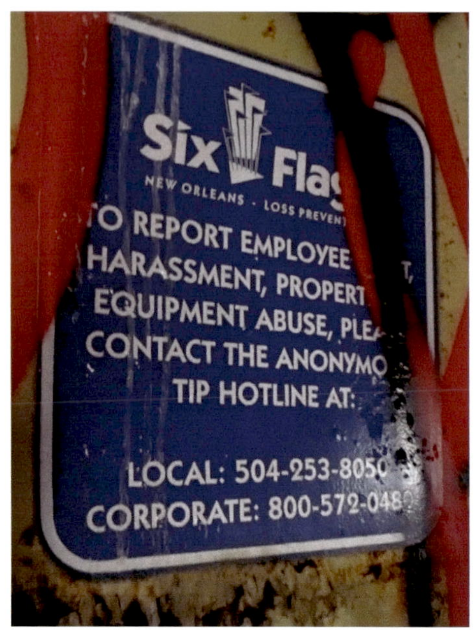

Above left: The once-majestic swing ride called The Zydeco Zinger now hangs lifeless, its few remaining chains swaying in the wind. Decorated panels that once added a touch of whimsy are now weathered and faded. To this day, this remains one of my most favorite subjects to photograph in the park.

Above right: While exploring, we found a faded employee sign still attached to one of the doors that opens into the park's recreation of the Orpheum Theatre.

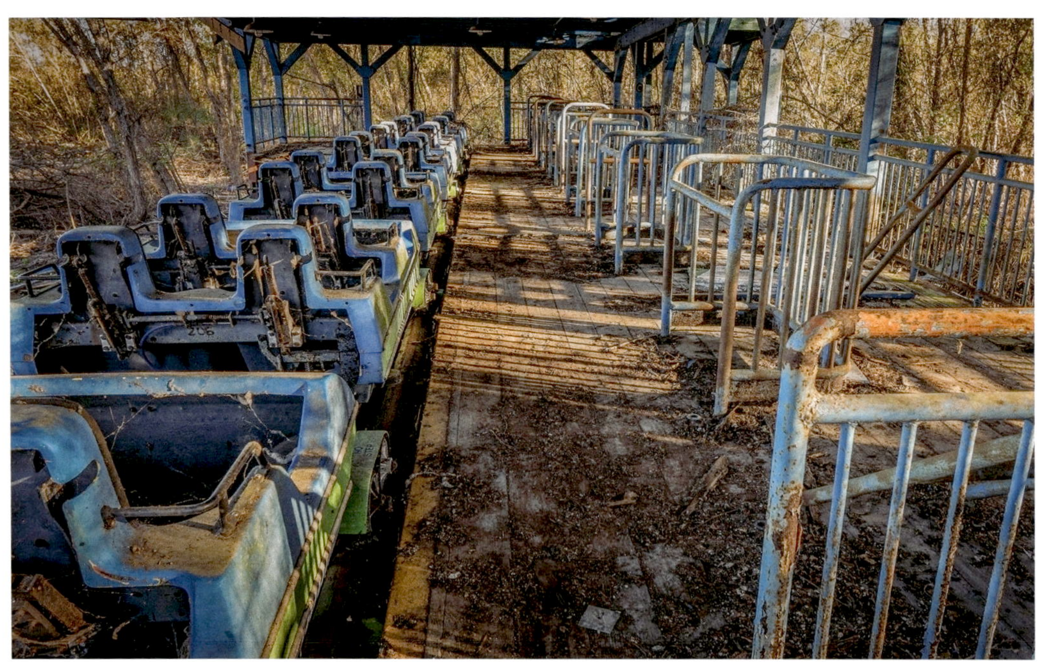

The Jester's coaster cars remain frozen on the track, their vibrant paint faded and frames covered in rust. The station, once bustling with excited riders, now lies in disrepair, overtaken by dirt and debris.

2

THE MARKET STREET POWER PLANT

An Industrial Giant Left Behind

In the early twentieth century, as New Orleans grew, the demand for electricity surged. To meet this need, the Market Street Power Plant was constructed in 1905. Located on the banks of the Mississippi River, the plant was strategically positioned to harness the river and serve the rapidly expanding city.

NOLA.com notes that it was originally designed to burn coal, powering the city's streetcars, homes, and businesses. Over the decades, the plant was expanded and modernized, switching from coal to oil, and later to natural gas as fuel. It became a crucial part of New Orleans' infrastructure, helping to light the city and drive its industrial growth.

The plant's architecture reflected the industrial might of the era, with its imposing brick facade, massive windows, and tall smokestacks that blew smoke into the sky. Inside, the plant housed giant turbines, boilers, and other machinery that hummed with the power that kept New Orleans running.

As the decades passed, however, the energy landscape began to change. New, more efficient power plants were being built, and the demand for electricity outgrew the capacity of older facilities like Market Street.

By the 1970s, the plant's technology had become outdated, and its operations were no longer economically viable. In 1973, after nearly seventy years of continuous operation, the power plant was decommissioned. The once-vital source of energy was now an industrial relic, its machinery silenced, and its future uncertain.

Following its closure, the building began to deteriorate. Its brick walls crumbling, and its steel structures rusting under the relentless Louisiana humidity.

The interior, once filled with the noise and activity of workers and machines, became a silent expanse of empty halls, littered with remnants of its industrial past.

It has since become a magnet for squatters, graffiti artists, and urban explorers, who are drawn to its eerie beauty. It has also been used in many film and television productions. The plant's massive scale, combined with its dilapidated state, gives it an almost otherworldly atmosphere, a place where time seems to stand still.

This was a long-awaited exploration for the krewe. One visit was not enough for us to capture everything, so we ventured inside on four separate occasions. The site was extremely dangerous, and we were fully aware of the risks lurking around every corner. During one visit, a member of the krewe accidentally stepped backward into a water-filled hole and fell in. Fortunately, he avoided the jagged, rusted metal hidden beneath the surface. While his camera took a hit and his pride took a bigger one, he emerged drenched but otherwise unscathed.

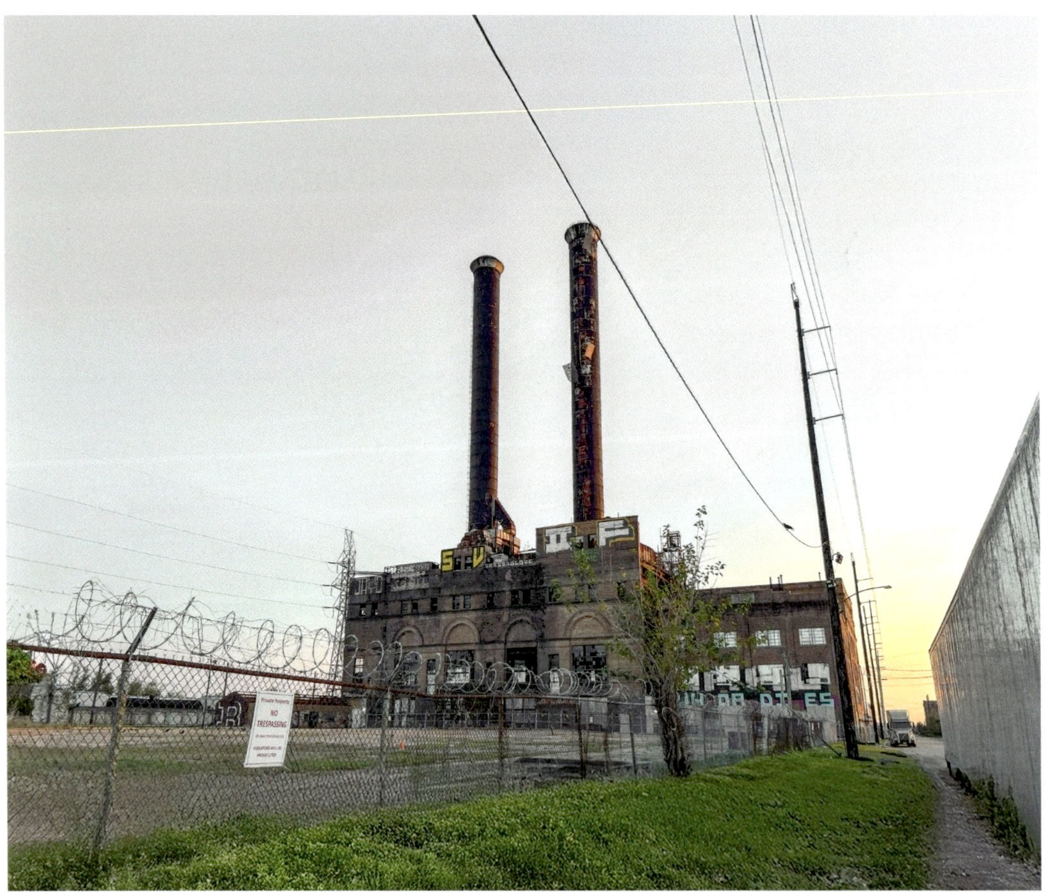

The Market Street Power Plant, built in 1905, once powered the city of New Orleans. Deserted since the 1970s, its towering smokestacks and crumbling facade are reminders of the city's industrial past.

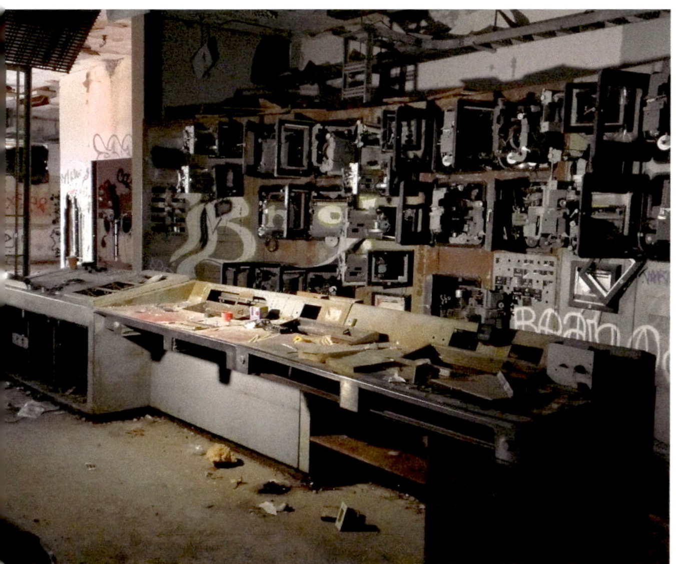
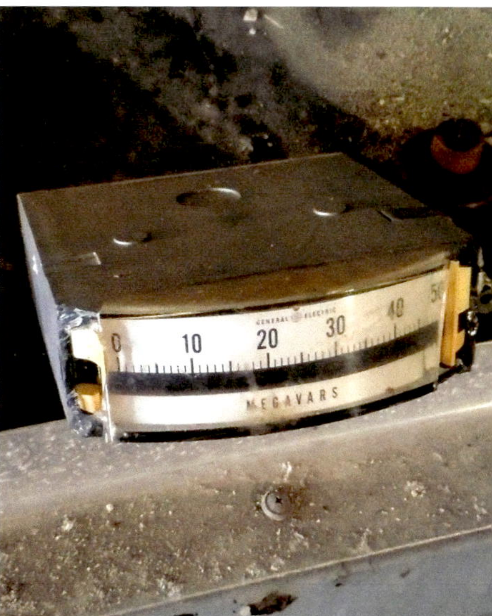

Above left: The control room of the power plant is now just a shadow of its former self. Broken panels, scattered debris, and graffiti contrast what was once the beating heart of the city's power grid.

Above right: A dusty gauge rests among the ruins of the control room, its needle no longer functioning. This was once used to monitor megavars of electricity, which indicate the magnetic fields needed to sustain generators and motors in the plant.

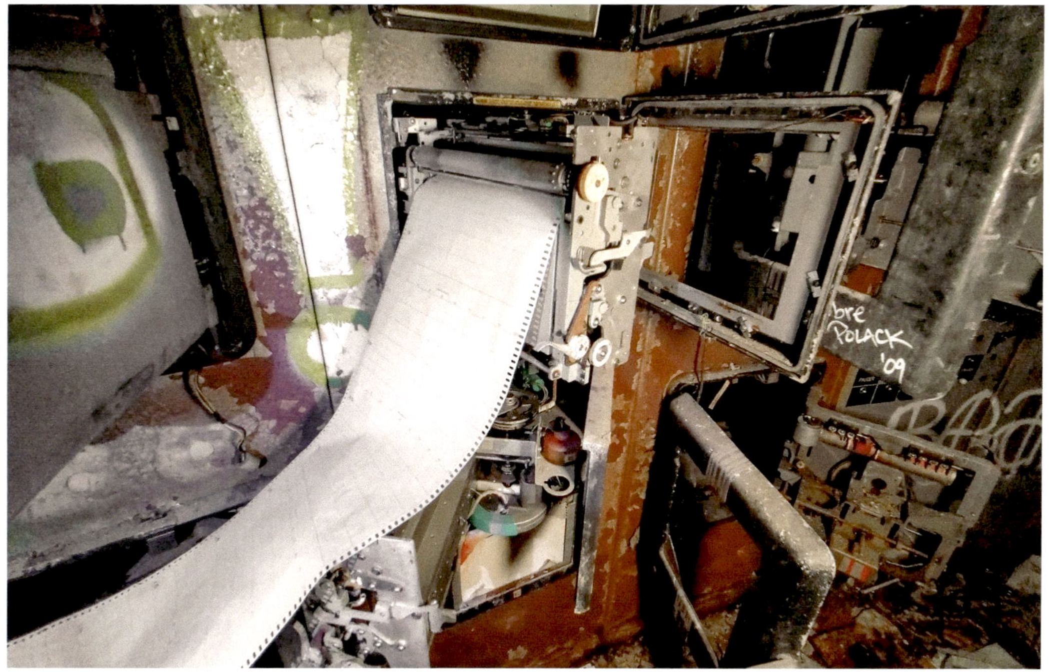

A chart recorder door dangles open, with old paper still loaded in it dating back to the 1970s when the plant was still in operation. This particular piece of equipment was used to monitor the plant's operations. Now it just sits collecting dust in the dim light.

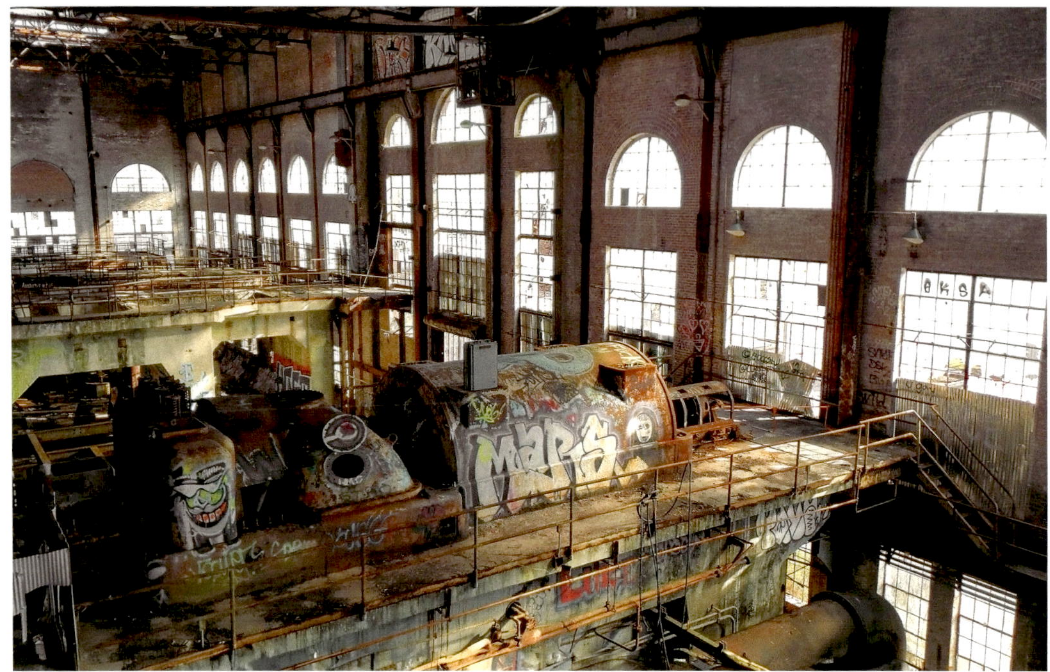

Sunlight streams through the beautiful broken windows, illuminating the rusty machinery inside. This cavernous space is now filled with silence, except for the echoes of our voices and footsteps. The last remaining turbine and peeling walls bear witness to many years of decay and vandalism.

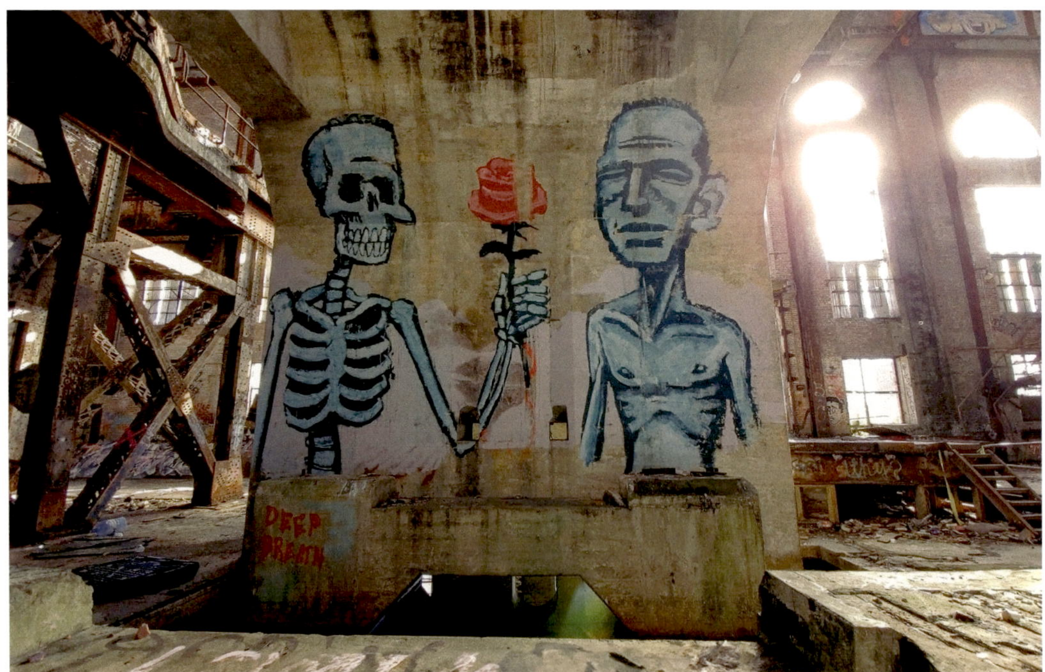

In the midst of all the rusty metal, an eye-catching mural brings a splash of life to the crumbling walls of the large room. A skeleton offers a rose to a solemn figure, a haunting yet hopeful gesture in a desolate space. The message of "Deep Breath" painted below is a poignant reminder to pause and reflect amid the ruin.

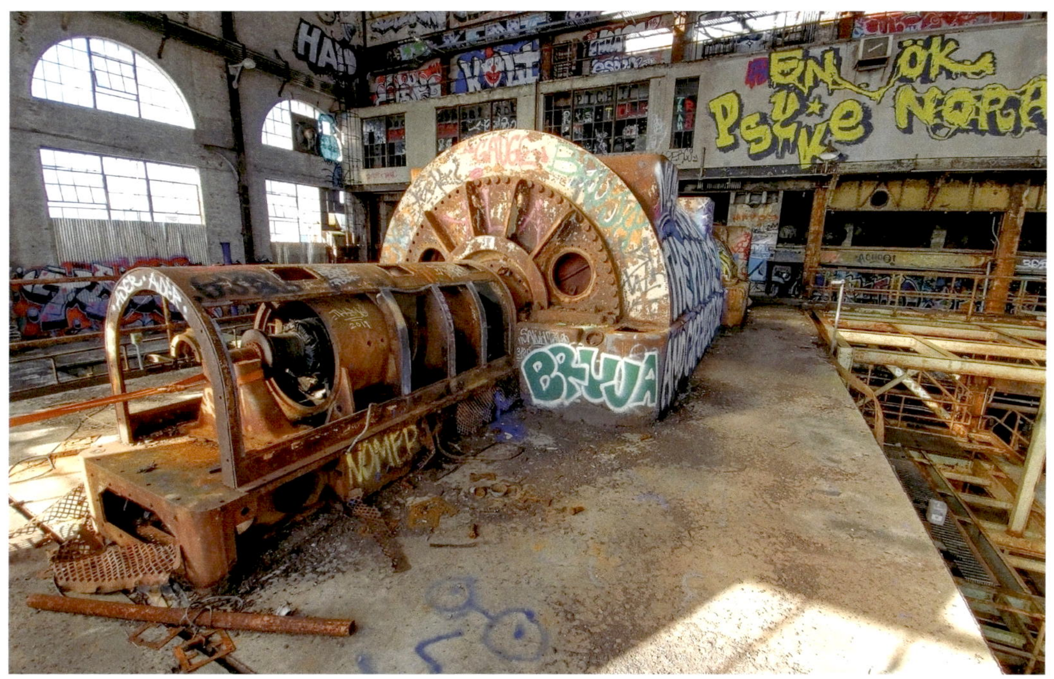

A closer look at one of the few remaining turbines that now lies silent and rusting away. Its insides are exposed to the elements, and it is surrounded by colorful urban art. The deserted room serves as a canvas for street artists, blending the past with the present.

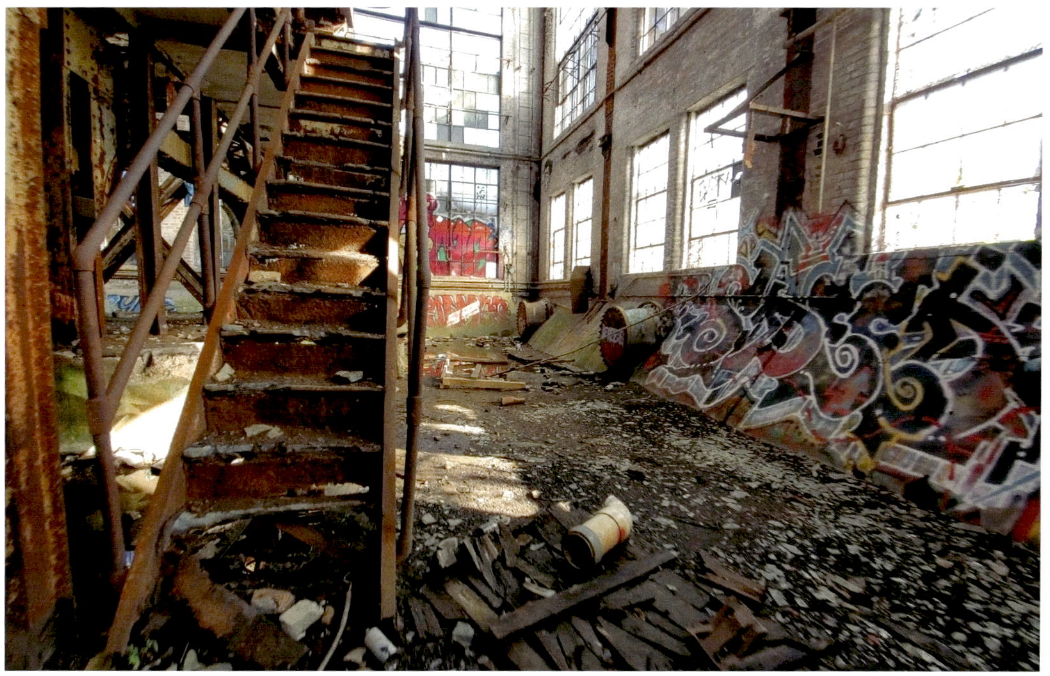

These rusty crumbling stairs lead up to the next floor, seemingly able to fall apart with every step. The krewe decided to use them anyway, albeit very carefully, to ascend upward. They were surprisingly, and thankfully, fairly sturdy underfoot.

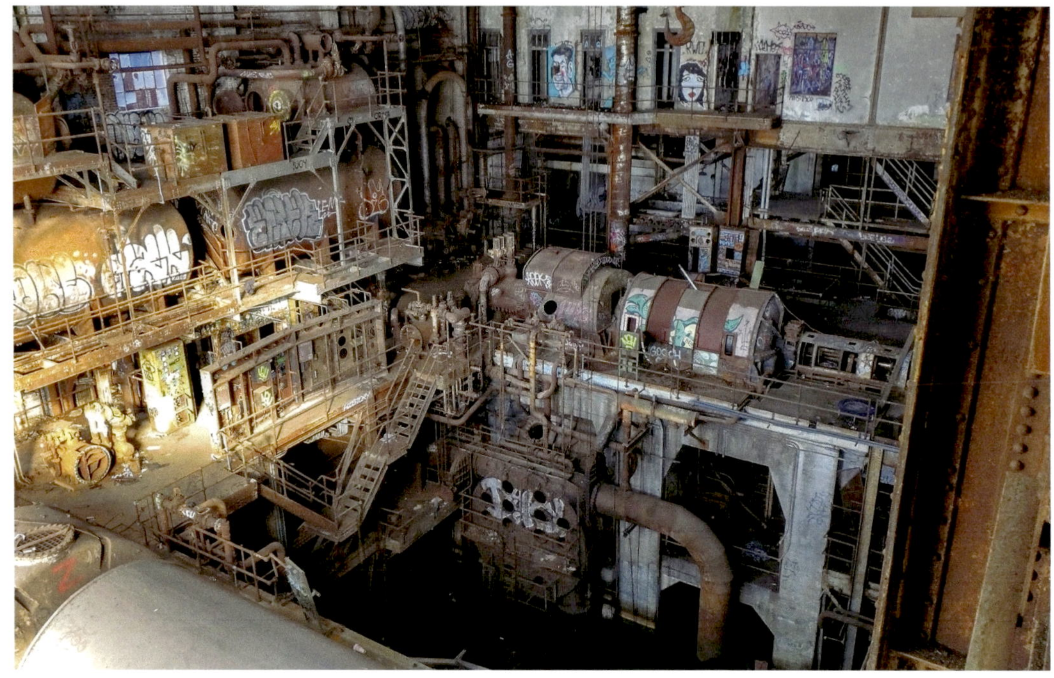

In the power plant's huge intake room, water from the Mississippi River was at one time used to cool the machinery vital to power production. More sunlight filters through what is left of the windows, illuminating the chaotic and dangerous maze of old rusty pipes, machinery, and rotting wooden catwalks.

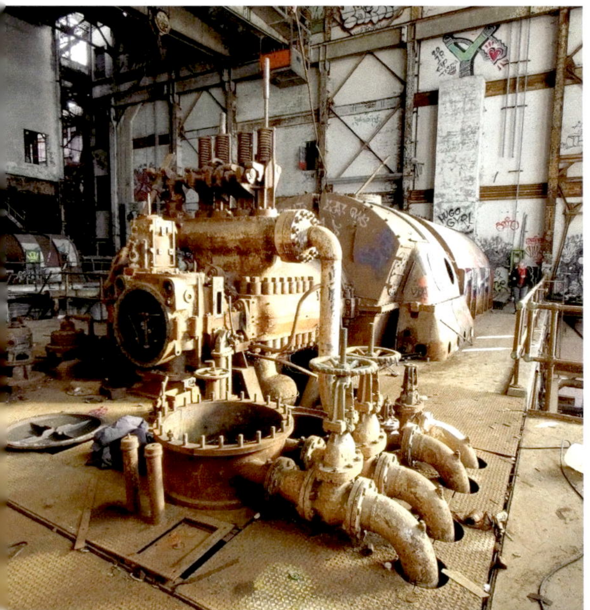

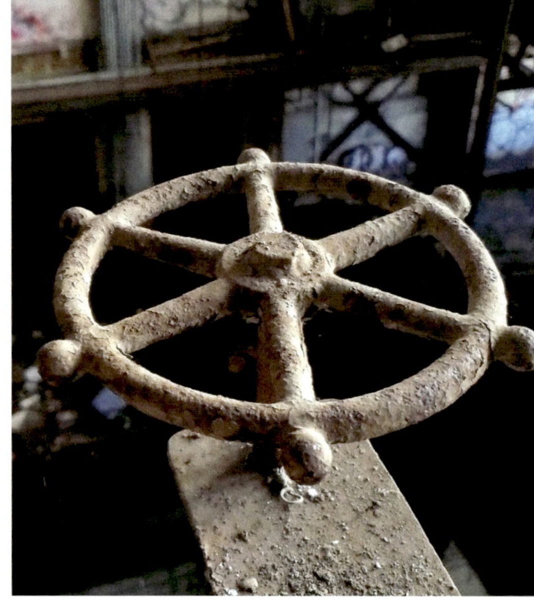

Above left: An old corroded turbine and valve assembly stand like relics of a bygone era. Once vital to powering the city, the machines now lie dormant, surrounded by graffiti-covered walls and the whispers of the past.

Above right: A rusty valve wheel overlooks the water intake area. It was a part of the plant's essential equipment, but now it is just a relic of the past. I attempted to turn it, but found time and rust had frozen it still.

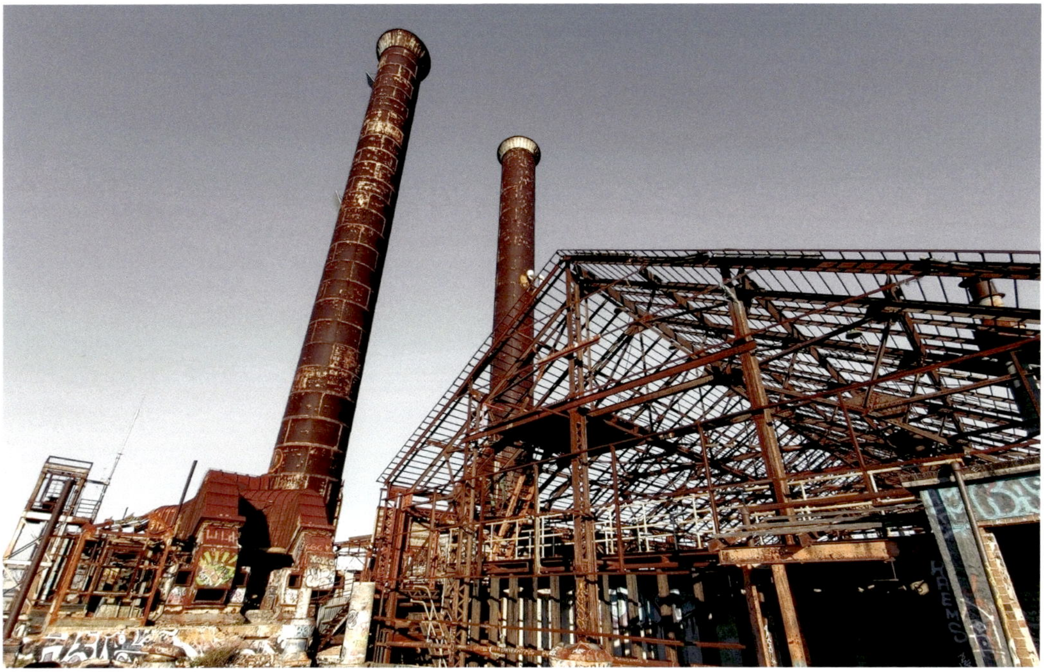

We made our way to the roof of the building to find the skeletal remains of the old exhaust equipment. The towering smokestacks, weathered by time, surprisingly still stand tall, bearing witness to decades of industrial evolution in the city.

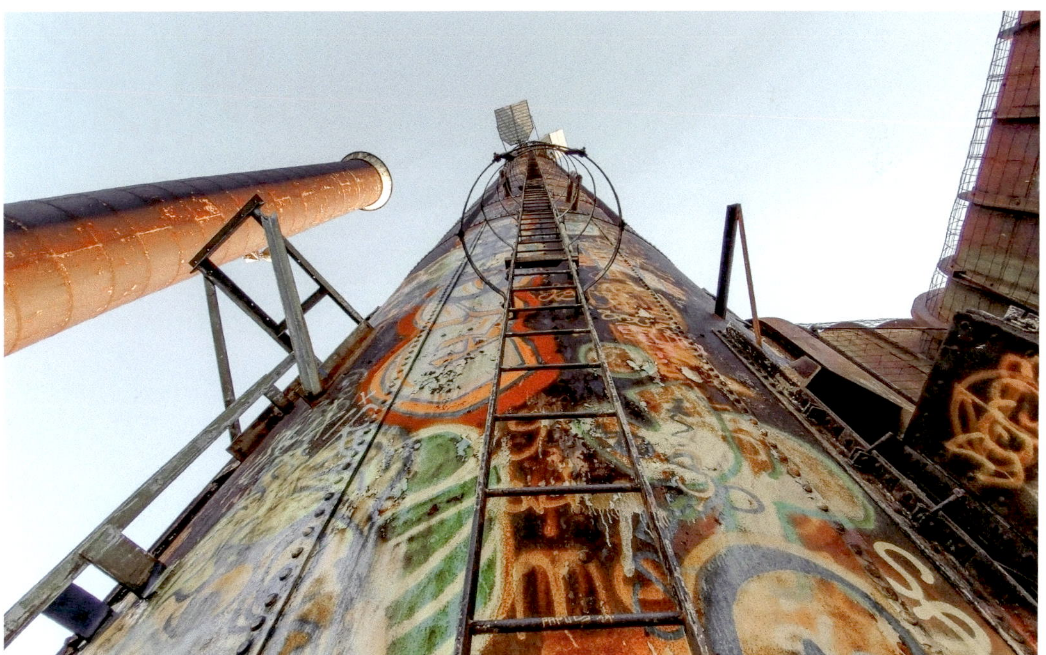

A vertigo-inducing view up one of the towering smokestacks. Once belching smoke as an integral part of the plant, it now stands aged and covered in layers of graffiti and rust, with its disintegrating ladder tempting only the most adventurous to climb.

3

PLAZA TOWER

New Orleans' Lofty Dream Turned Silent Sentinel

Construction began on Plaza Tower in 1964, according to the Preservation Resource Center of New Orleans. When the tower was completed in 1969, it became the tallest building in Louisiana. The forty-five-story skyscraper would house offices, luxury apartments, and commercial spaces, offering a mix of residential and business amenities in one prime location.

The building quickly became a desirable address for businesses and residents alike, attracting a mix of corporate offices, law firms, and high-end tenants. Its location, just outside the Central Business District, offered easy access to downtown while providing stunning views of the Mississippi River and the city below.

The tower's design and height made it a landmark, visible from miles away, and it was seen as a testament to New Orleans' aspirations as a modern, forward-looking city. However, beneath the surface, problems were beginning to emerge that would ultimately lead to the tower's downfall.

By the 1980s, the tower's initial luster had begun to fade. The building was aging, and maintenance issues were becoming more pronounced. The most significant problem, per NOLA.com, was the discovery of asbestos. Asbestos, once commonly used for its fire-resistant properties, was by then recognized as a serious health hazard, linked to lung cancer and other respiratory illnesses.

Removal or containment would be costly and complicated, and as concerns about the building's safety grew, tenants began to leave. By the late 1990s, the tower was largely vacant, and in 2002, the last tenants moved out, leaving it completely empty.

Despite various proposals to repurpose the building, including plans to convert it into luxury condominiums, none came to fruition.

In early 2020, a significant chunk of debris dislodged from the upper levels of the building, crashing onto the streets below. Fortunately, no injuries were reported, but several vehicles sustained damage. This incident prompted an immediate closure of the surrounding roads as city officials acted swiftly to safeguard pedestrians and motorists from potential hazards.

In response, the decision was made to install protective netting around the top of the structure to capture any additional loose debris that might fall. The streets remained closed until the netting was completely in place, allowing for a safer reopening to traffic and pedestrians. However, the netting was perceived as a temporary measure, and public anxiety regarding long-term safety continued to escalate.

In August 2021, Hurricane Ida struck, and the fierce winds inflicted damage on the netting. A new net was added which has remained in place ever since. Caught between the high costs of redevelopment or demolition and the risks associated with its structural and environmental issues, it remains a part of the city's skyline.

The krewe had been planning to explore the skyscraper for a while, and the day finally came for us to make it happen. We carefully made our way through the forty-five-story building, floor by floor. Each level revealed its own collection of graffiti and remnants left behind by squatters. About halfway up, we even discovered an old rooftop pool. While most of the building was empty, the view of New Orleans from high above in a deserted skyscraper was an unforgettable experience.

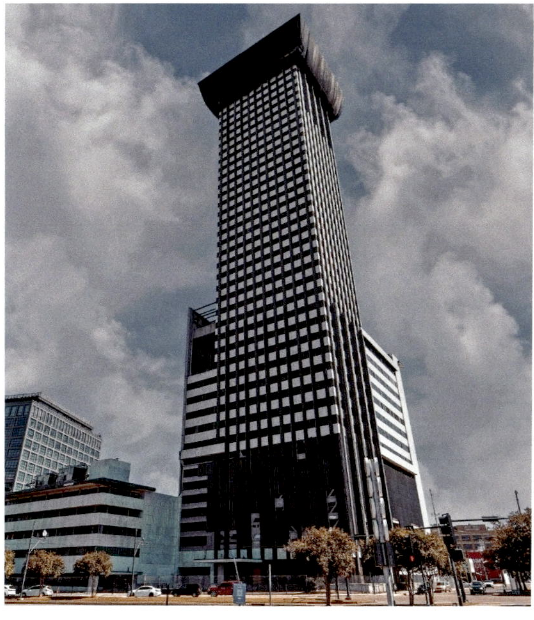

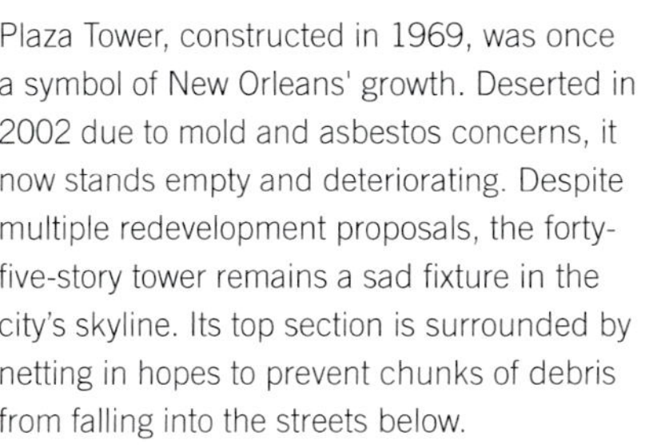

Plaza Tower, constructed in 1969, was once a symbol of New Orleans' growth. Deserted in 2002 due to mold and asbestos concerns, it now stands empty and deteriorating. Despite multiple redevelopment proposals, the forty-five-story tower remains a sad fixture in the city's skyline. Its top section is surrounded by netting in hopes to prevent chunks of debris from falling into the streets below.

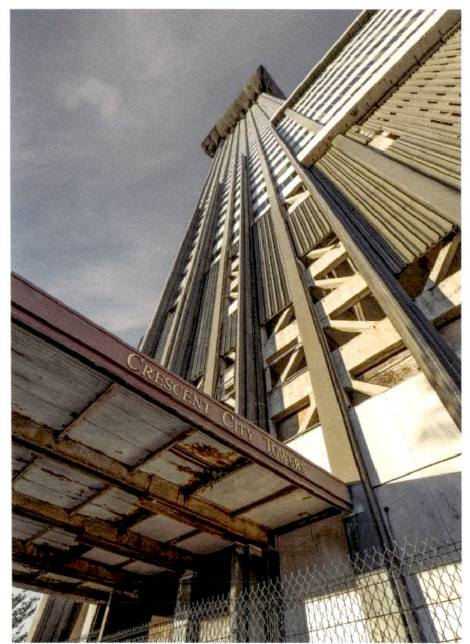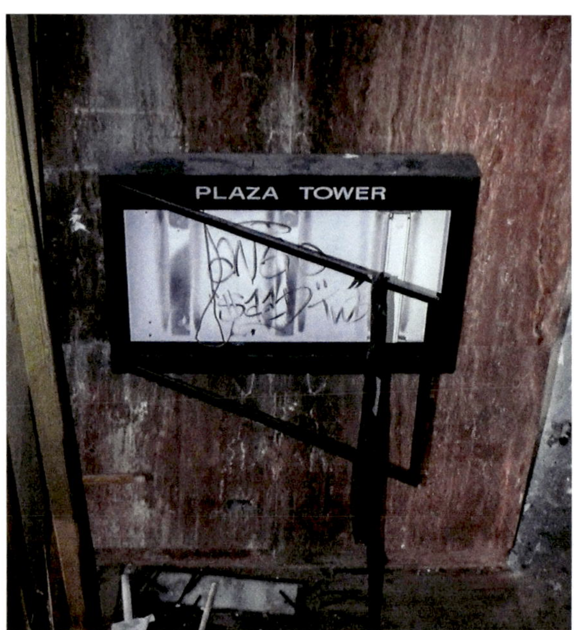

Above left: Over the years, Plaza Tower went through several name changes. A sign for "Crescent City Towers" is still part of the decaying entrance.

Above right: Inside the old building, on the first floor, there is a broken directory sign. Though now obscured with graffiti, it serves as a reminder of the tower's former glory days.

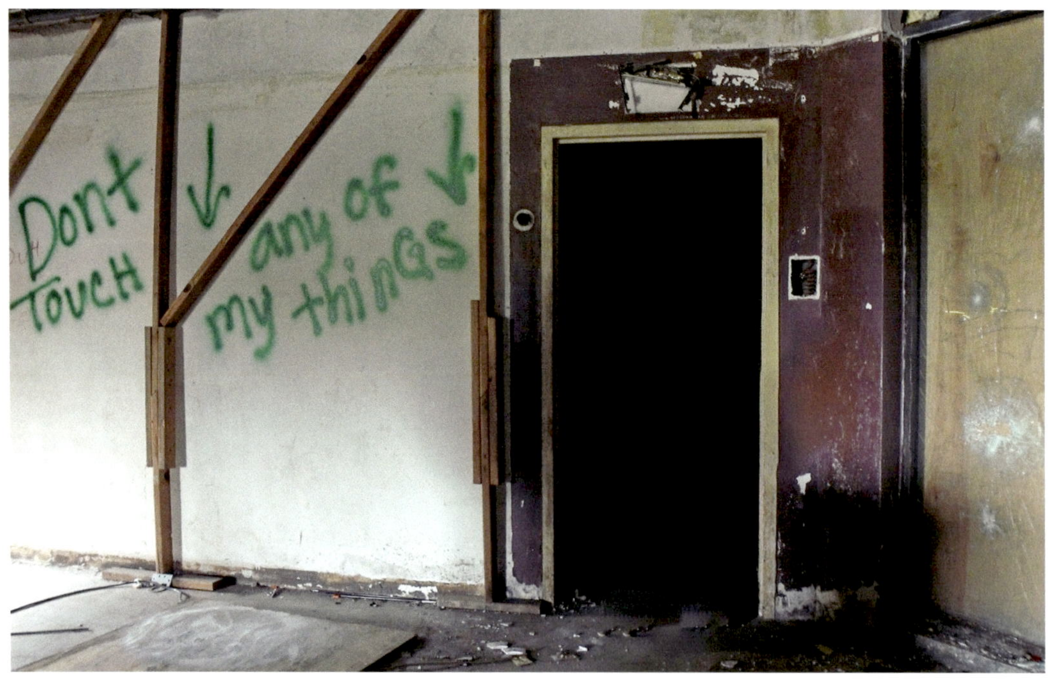

As the krewe ascended each floor, we found various signs of squatters living inside the huge building. On one of the floors, we found a foreboding message scrawled on a wall that reads, "don't touch any of my things," marking a territorial area for one of the building's occupants.

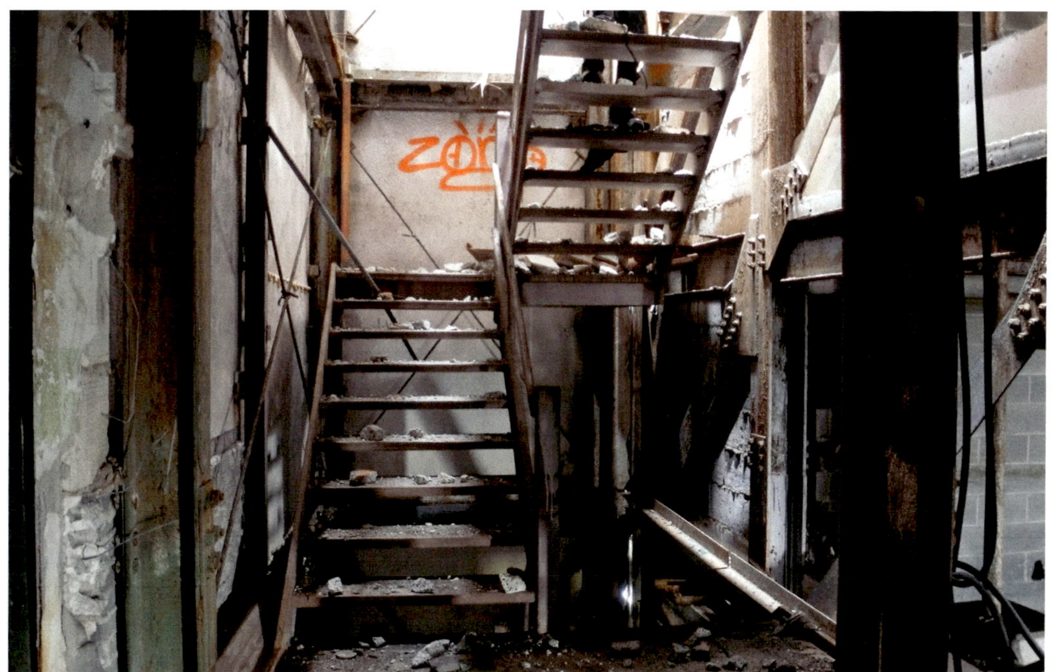

An old rickety staircase, covered in debris and rust, was the only way we could get up and down the huge skyscraper. In shape or not, climbing these questionable stairs was not an easy task for any of us in the krewe.

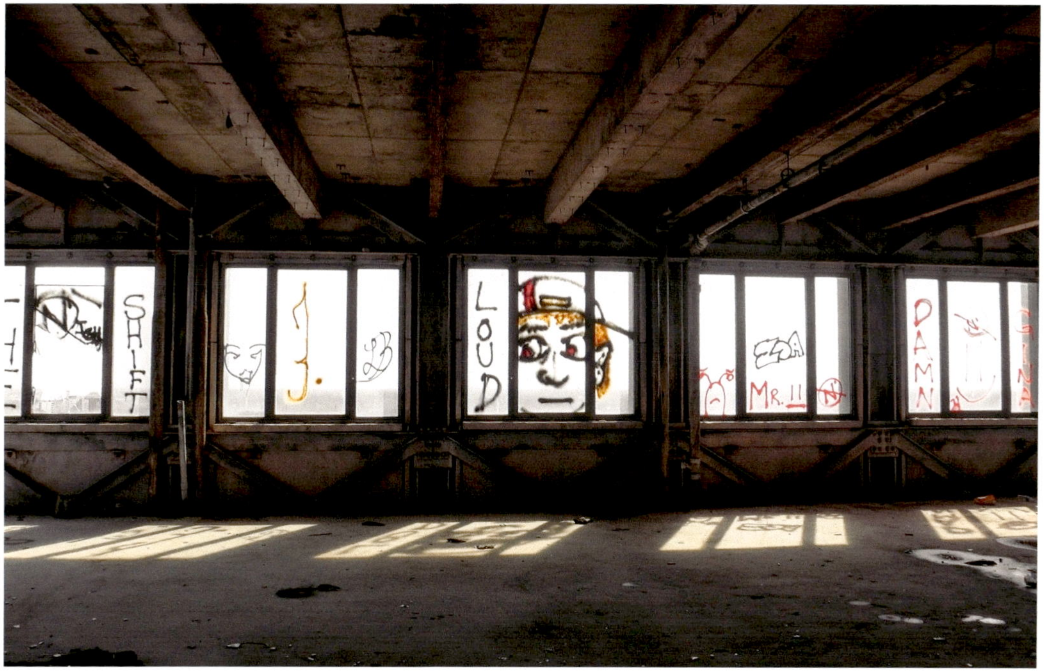

Graffiti fills these surprisingly intact windows of the old building, transforming the once pristine panes into a canvas of cryptic messages and faces.

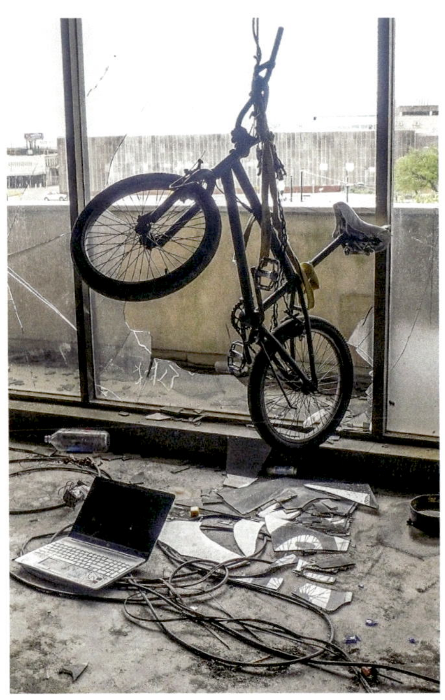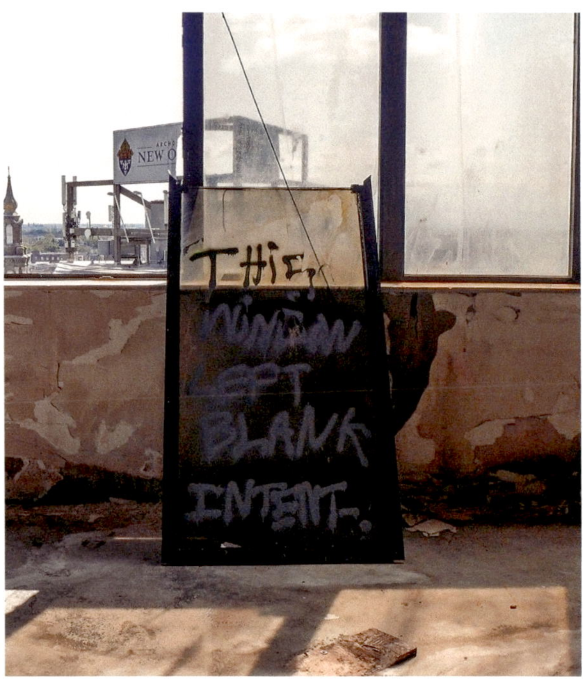

Above left: A surreal scene inside the tower many floors up: a bicycle dangles mysteriously by its handlebars, while a shattered laptop lies among broken glass and debris. The remnants of someone's life or a fleeting attempt to leave a mark. The shattered windows offer a view of the city outside, contrasting the makeshift dwelling within.

Above right: A single windowpane leans against the wall, tagged with the cryptic message: "this window left blank intent-." The walls and harsh sunlight pouring in highlight the contrast between the decaying interior and the bustling city outside. It is as if the building is slowly revealing its secrets while the world outside moves on.

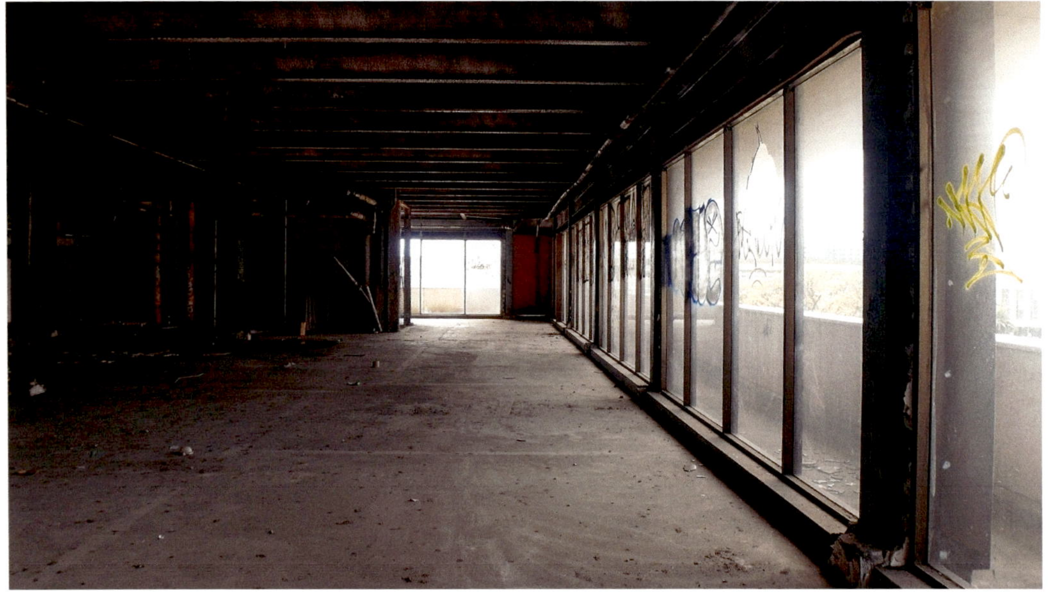

A desolate floor where natural light seeps through the dirty windows. The emptiness of this vast, deserted space is haunting, with only the occasional scribble of spray paint breaking the monotony.

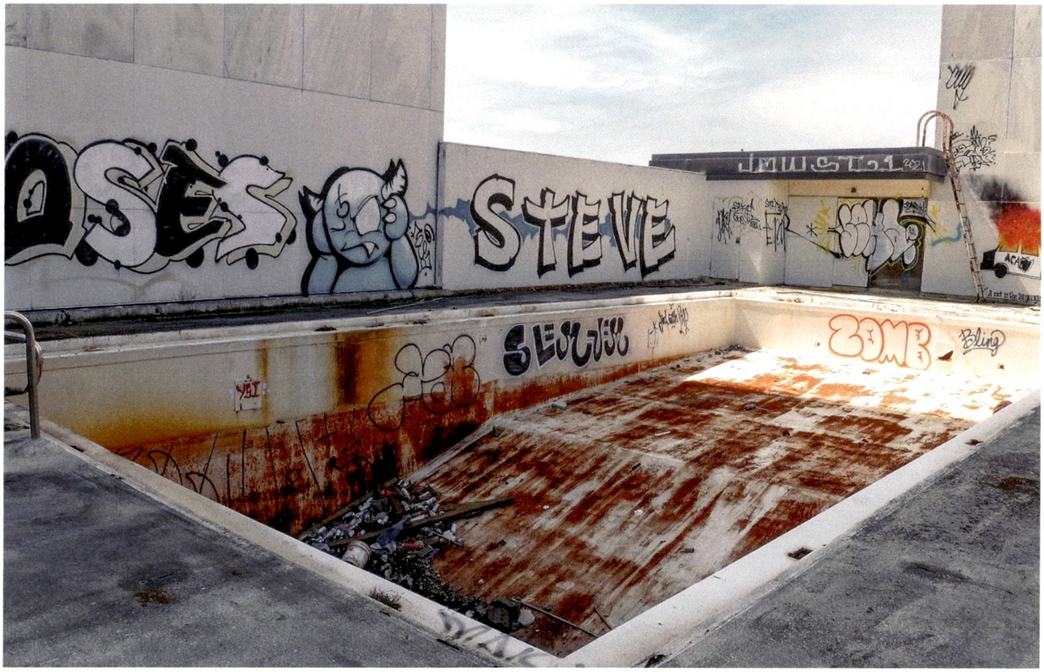

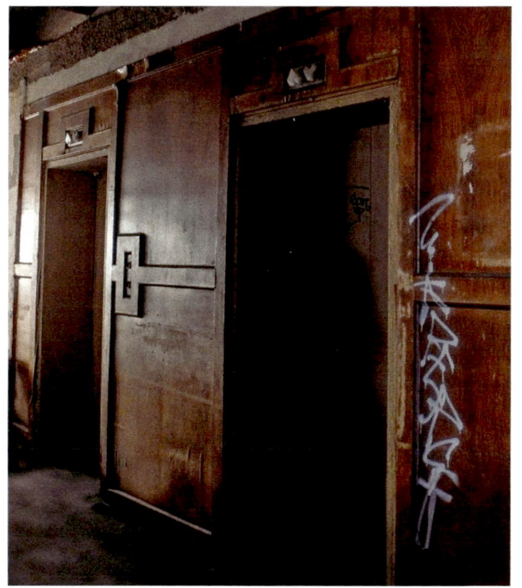

Halfway up, we discovered an empty rooftop pool filled with rust and debris. Now empty, it was once likely a lively spot for sunbathers. The vibrant spray-painted artwork surrounding it tells the story of others who have come and gone, leaving their mark on the walls of this forgotten space.

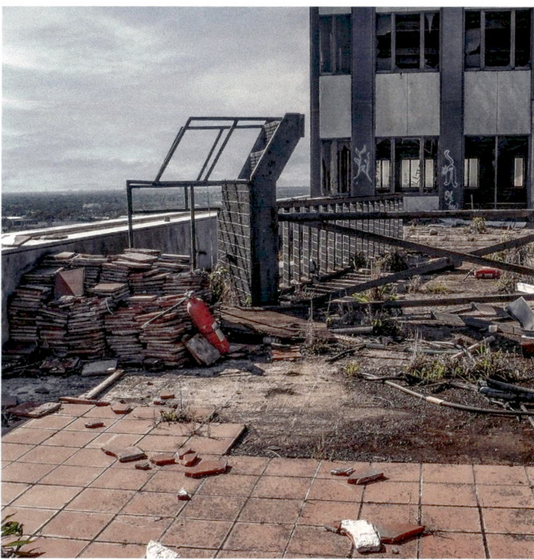

Above left: The wooden paneling of one of the elevator lobbies high up in the tower now stands marred by the passage of time. These old elevators, frozen in time, were the means of travel to the offices or living areas located in the building.

Above right: While exploring, we stumbled upon a small balcony on one of the higher floors of the building, likely an outside dining area. We imagined what it must have been like to sit out here while eating a delicious sandwich overlooking the Mississippi River and city below.

4

THE F. EDWARD HEBERT DEFENSE COMPLEX

The Navy's Forgotten Fortress

The F. Edward Hebert Defense Complex is located in New Orleans' Marigny neighborhood. This complex, known for its role as a Naval Support Activity (NSA) facility, now sits deserted.

The Preservation Resource Center of New Orleans says that construction began during World War I. As the United States ramped up its military efforts to support the war in Europe, the need for robust logistical and support infrastructure became evident. The location on Poland Avenue was chosen for its proximity to the Mississippi River and the Port of New Orleans, which were crucial for the transportation of troops, equipment, and supplies.

The complex was initially established as a naval depot, providing vital support to the navy's operations during the war. Its strategic importance grew over the years, and by the time of World War II, the facility had expanded to accommodate a wider range of military activities, solidifying its status as a key naval installation.

In the following decades, it evolved into a critical center for the navy's NSA. It housed a wide array of services, including personnel training, equipment maintenance, and communications, making it an indispensable asset to the navy's regional operations.

The complex was not just a military installation but also a small, self-contained community. It featured housing for military families, recreational facilities, and other amenities that created a sense of camaraderie among those stationed there.

As the Cold War came to an end, the need for large-scale support facilities like this began to diminish. Advances in technology and changes in military strategy led to a gradual reduction in the facility's operations. By the early 2000s, the navy had begun to downsize its presence in New Orleans, and the complex was no longer seen as essential and in 2009, the decision was made to close the facility permanently.

The sprawling complex has since served as the backdrop for numerous film and television productions. Over time, it has also become a hub for illicit activities, including drug deals, violence, and even as a site for hiding evidence of crimes. Squatters often take refuge within its many accessible areas, and despite periodic city efforts to secure and clear the property, it is usually reclaimed within days.

Out of all the deserted places in New Orleans, this one drew us back repeatedly. Its massive size offered endless spaces to explore and document, and each of our six visits revealed something new and fascinating. Our favorite discovery though was a theater room, where the seats remained intact and the projector screen still in place, a rare and haunting sight.

Each visit, the krewe made sure to stick together, following a safety-in-numbers approach. With stories of robberies, violence, and drug activity circulating about this site, we took every precaution we could to navigate its dangers while uncovering its hidden history.

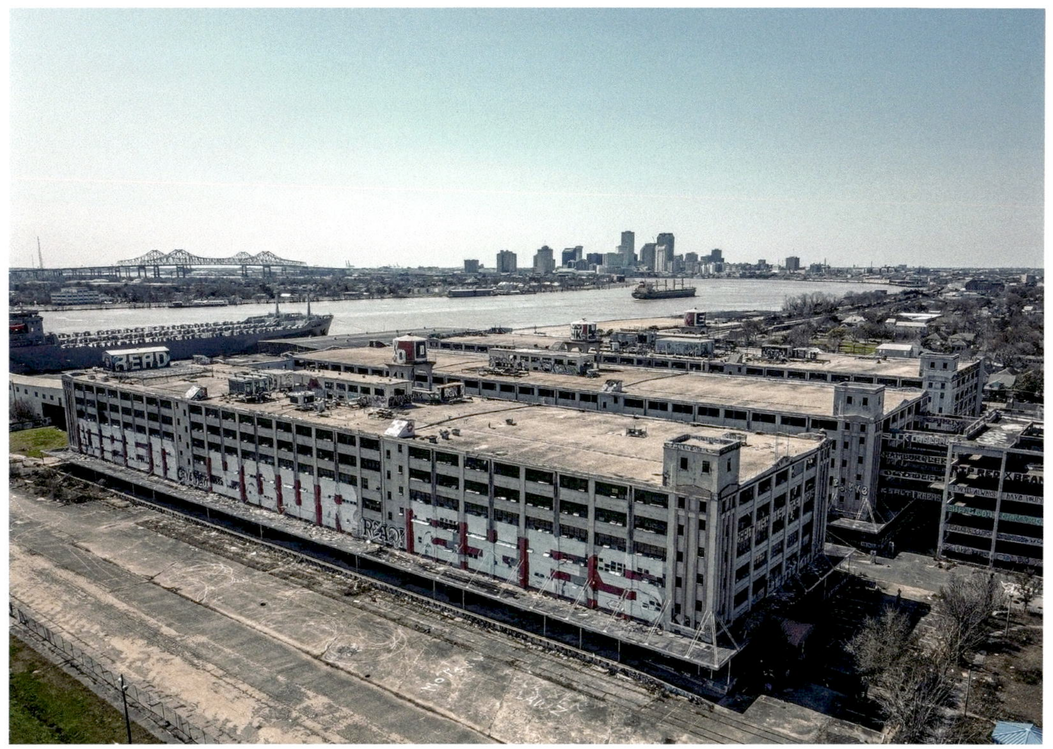

The F. Edward Hebert Defense Complex was constructed in the early 1900s. This sprawling complex supported navy operations through both world wars and was later repurposed during the Cold War. By 2009, the base was officially decommissioned, leaving it deserted.

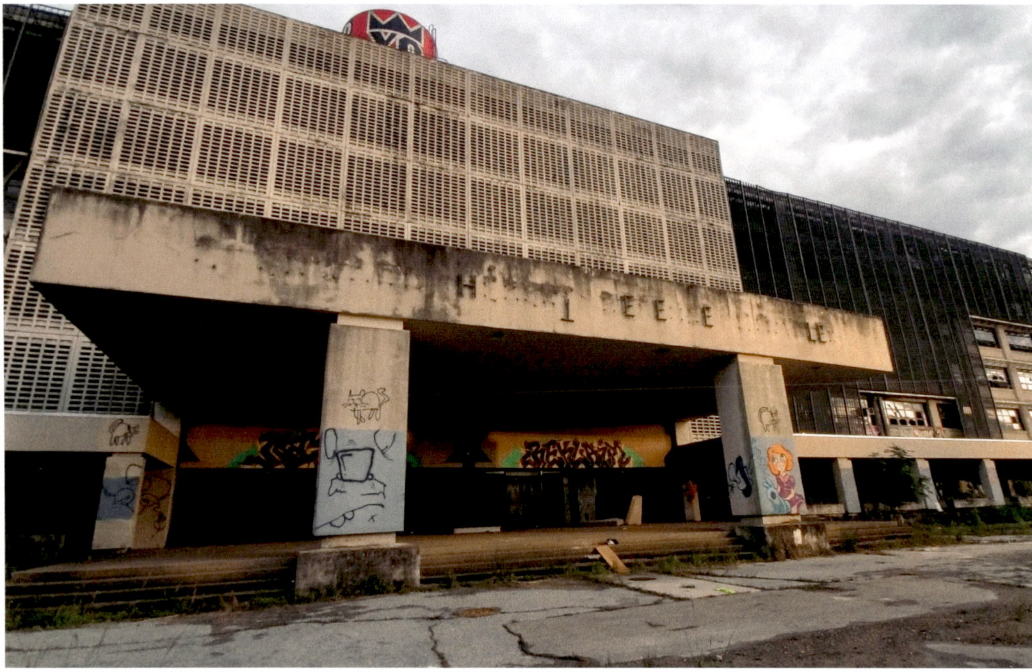

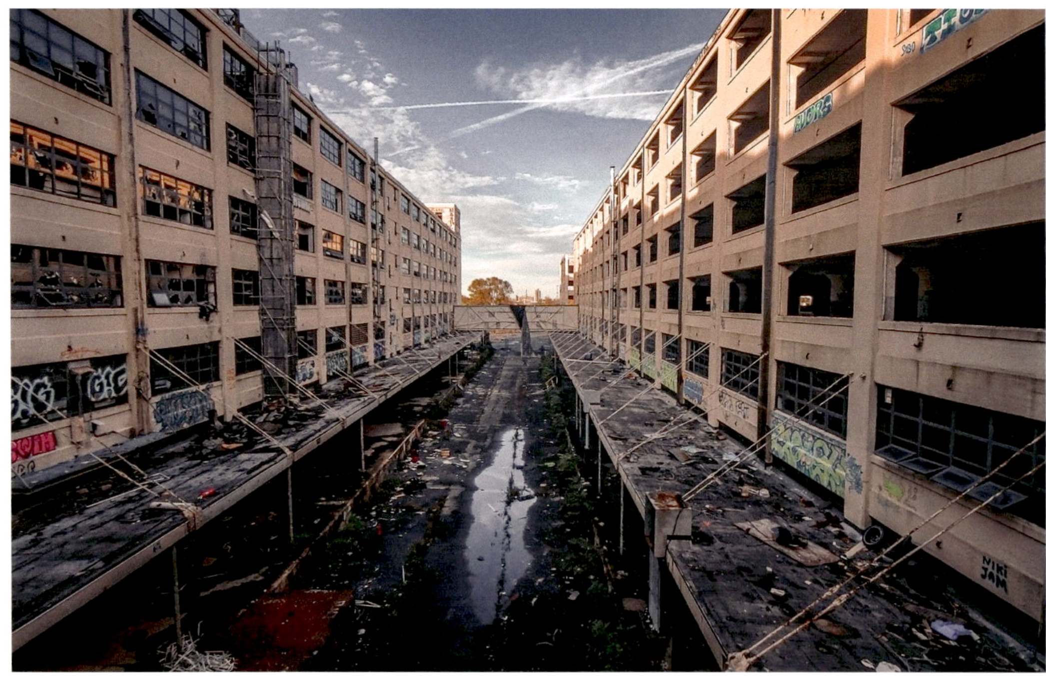

The weathered entrance of one of the former buildings. Faint letters that once read "F. Edward Hebert Defense Complex" hint at the site's past significance, while new tags and artwork mark the transition from military stronghold to urban canvas.

Flanked by decaying walls and shattered windows, an area between two of the buildings is strewn with debris and graffiti. It reflects the slow degradation of this once great complex by time and the elements.

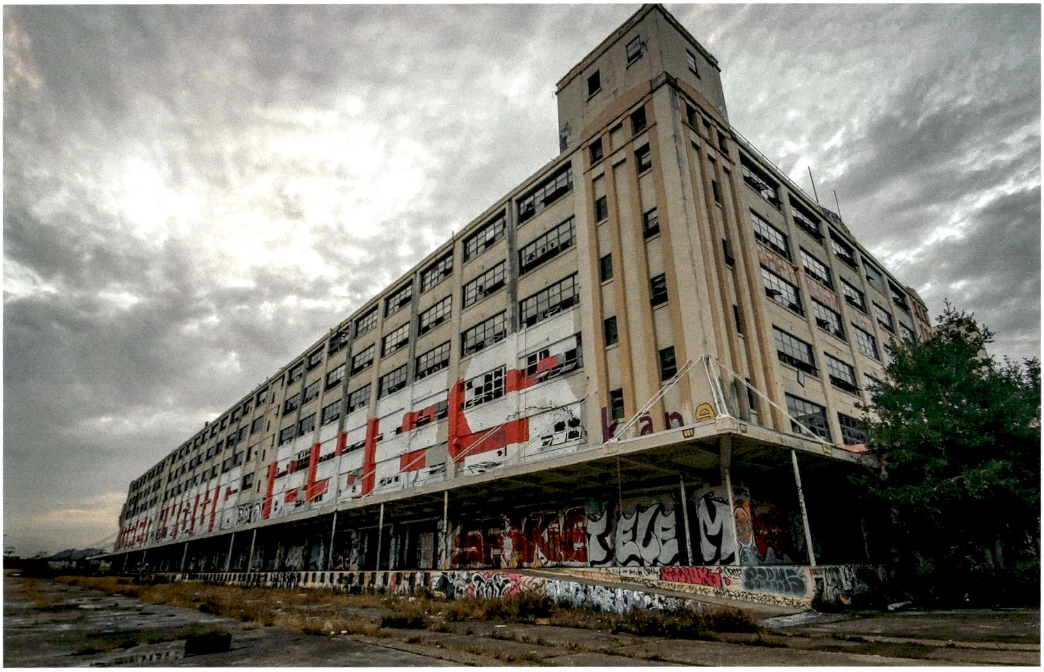

The large exterior of the complex stretches across the Mississippi River waterfront displaying the spray-painted message "open your eyes."

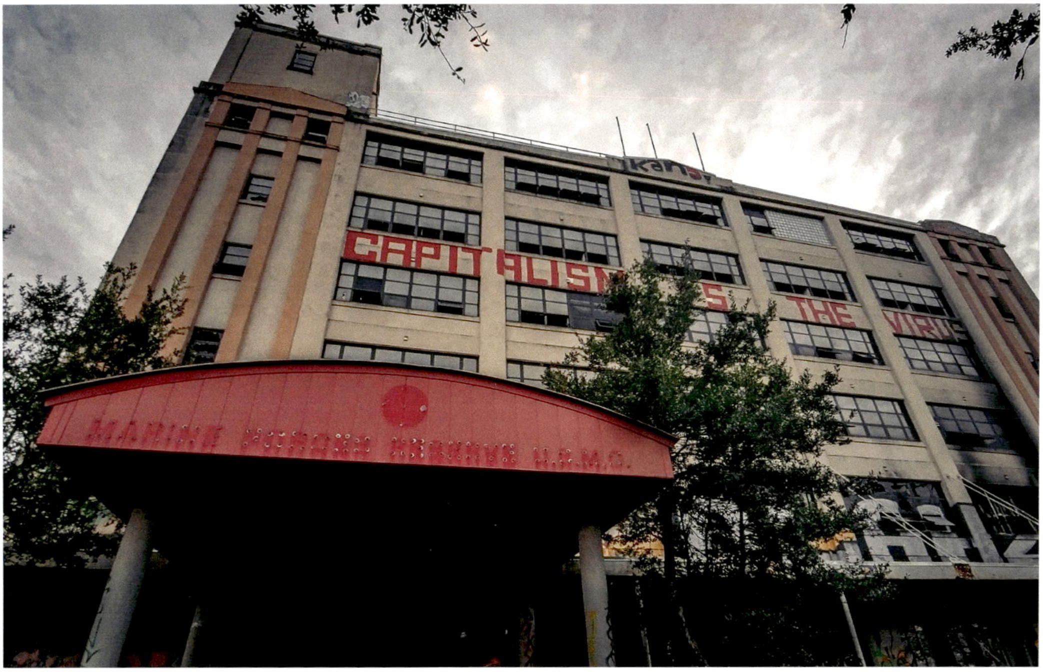

A faded awning that once read "Marine Forces Reserve, U.S.M.C." indicates the shared role this building played as part of the navy complex. Just above it, "capitalism is the virus" looms across its weathered facade, reflecting the building's transformation from a symbol of authority to a canvas for the city's rebellious spirit.

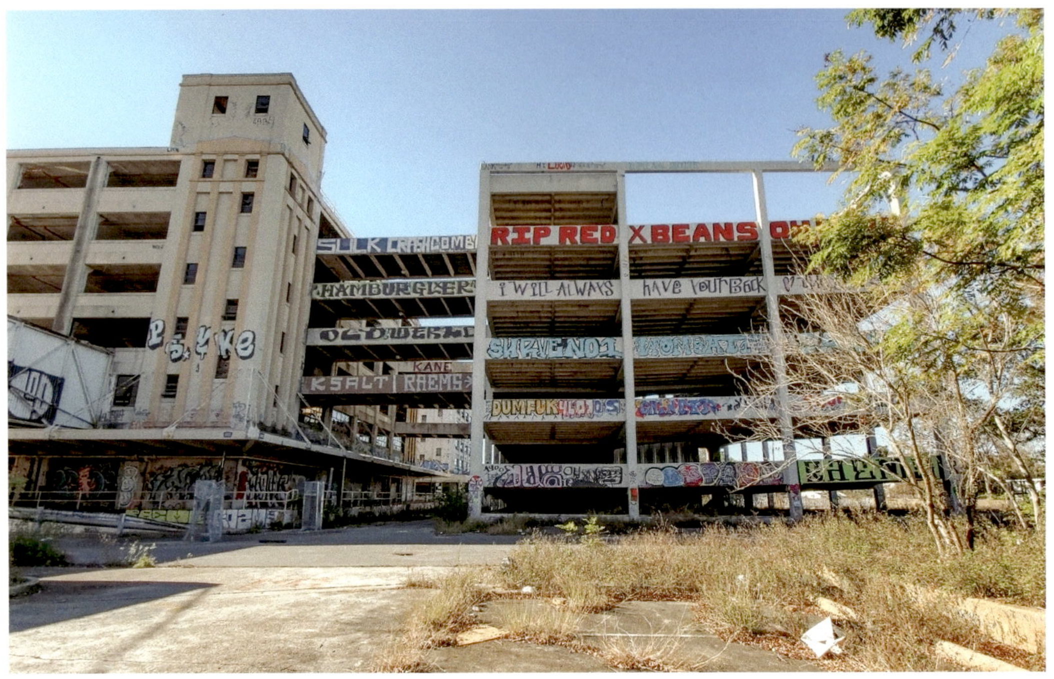

The old parking structure and ramp have become a graffiti artist's playground. Spray-paint artwork covers almost every surface with colorful messages and names left behind to be a mark of legacy.

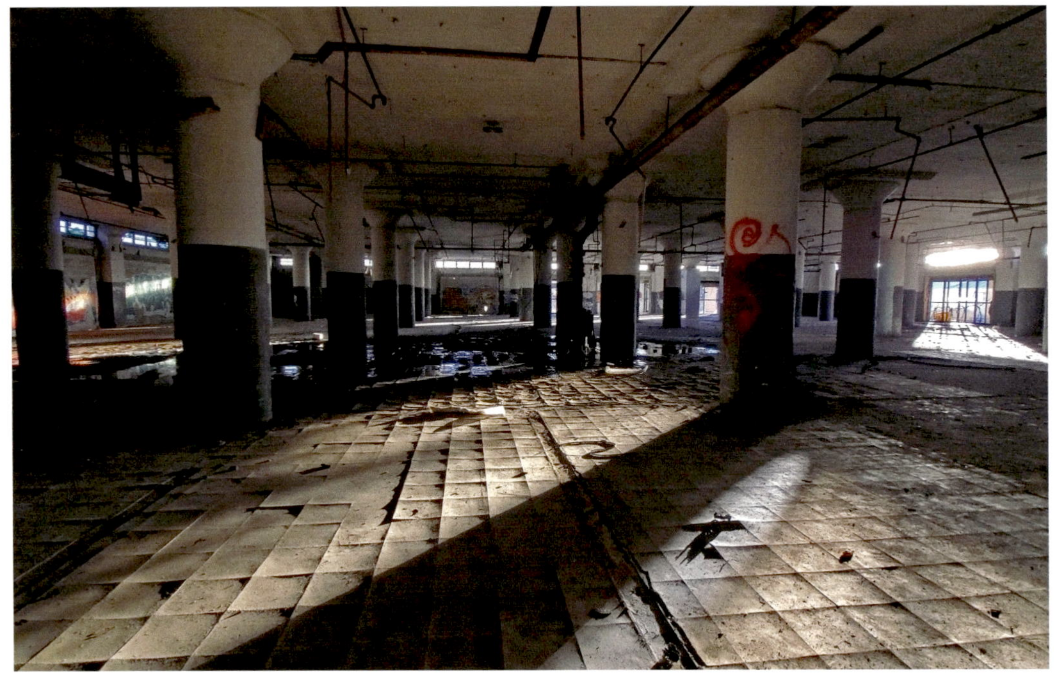

Inside, the sunlight filters through broken windows, casting shadows on the cracked tile floor. This large area is now empty, with remnants of old infrastructure hanging from the ceiling and walls.

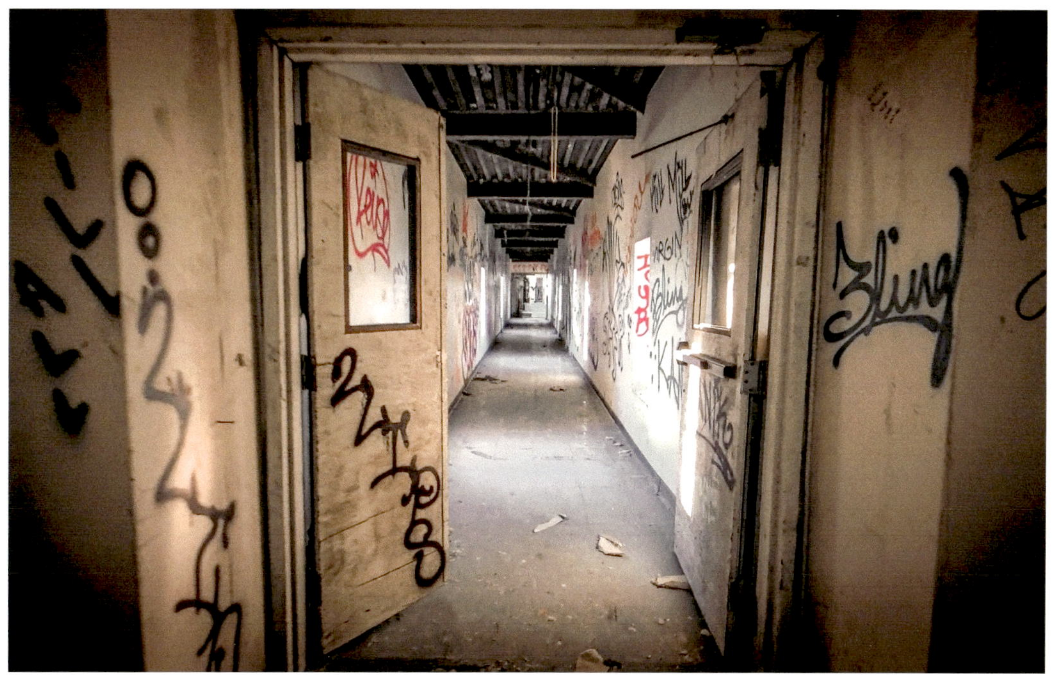

One of several narrow hallways that connects two of the buildings together is filled with broken doors and windows. The crude messages and tags on the walls add an unsettling atmosphere, turning this once orderly corridor into a chaotic, art-covered passage.

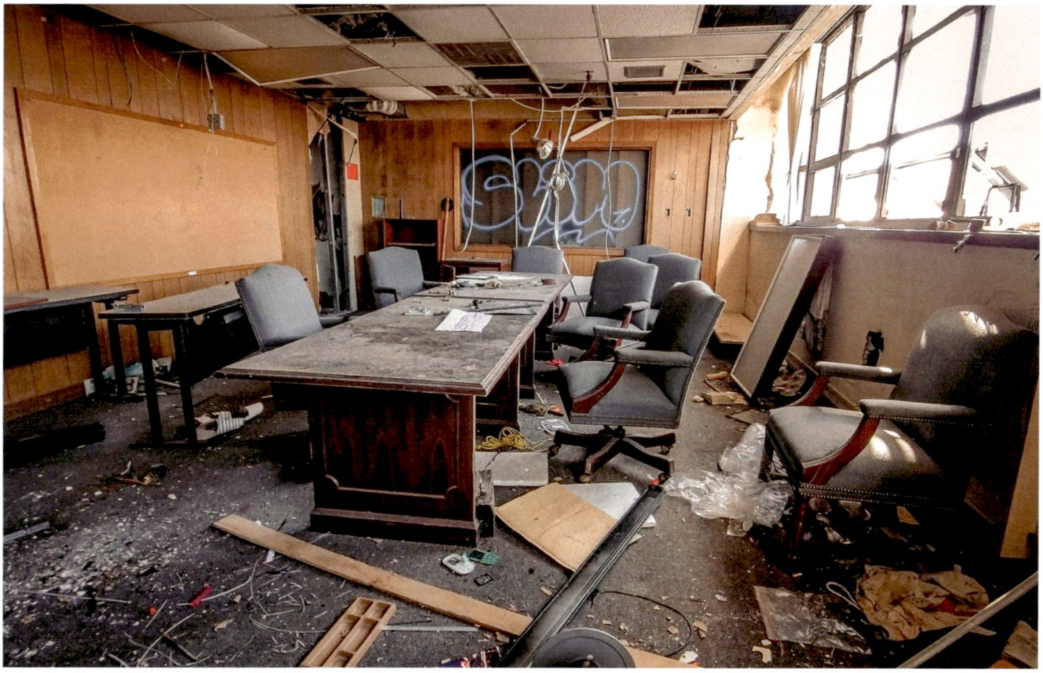

A conference room left in disarray inside one of the buildings. The room, likely used for many important meetings, is now littered with broken furniture, scattered papers, and debris.

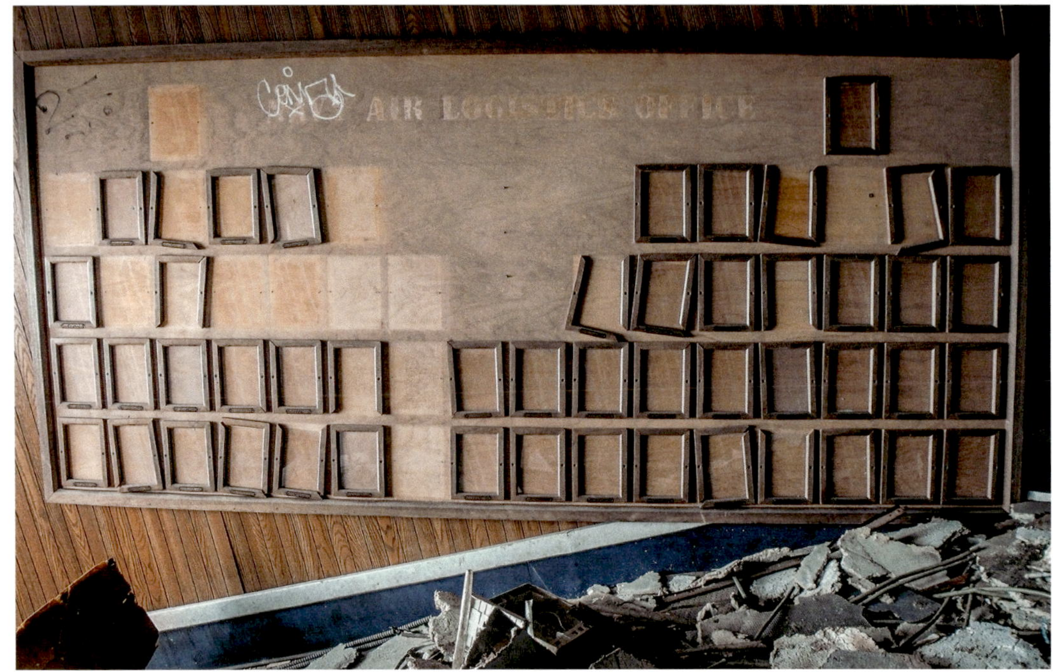

An old, empty directory board is missing all of its photos and name plates. At one time, it proudly displayed the names of offices and personnel specifically for the Air Logistics Office. Now it just serves as a silent reminder of the building's former occupants.

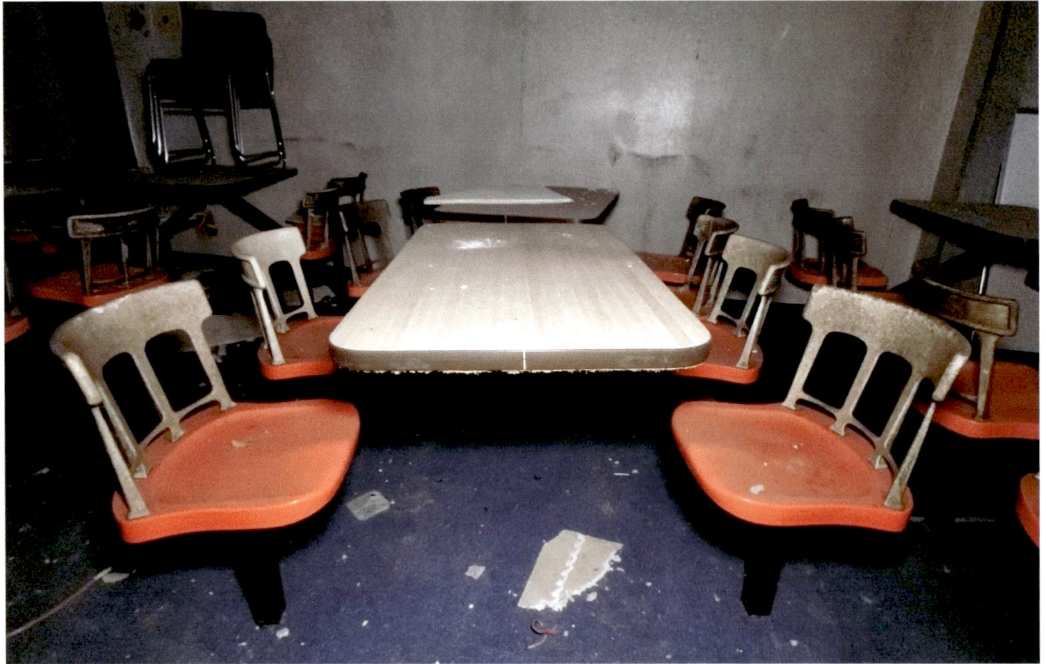

The mess area features faded orange chairs still bolted to the floor around worn-out tables. The room, now filled with dust and debris, was at one time a place for people to eat their meals while talking and laughing with one another.

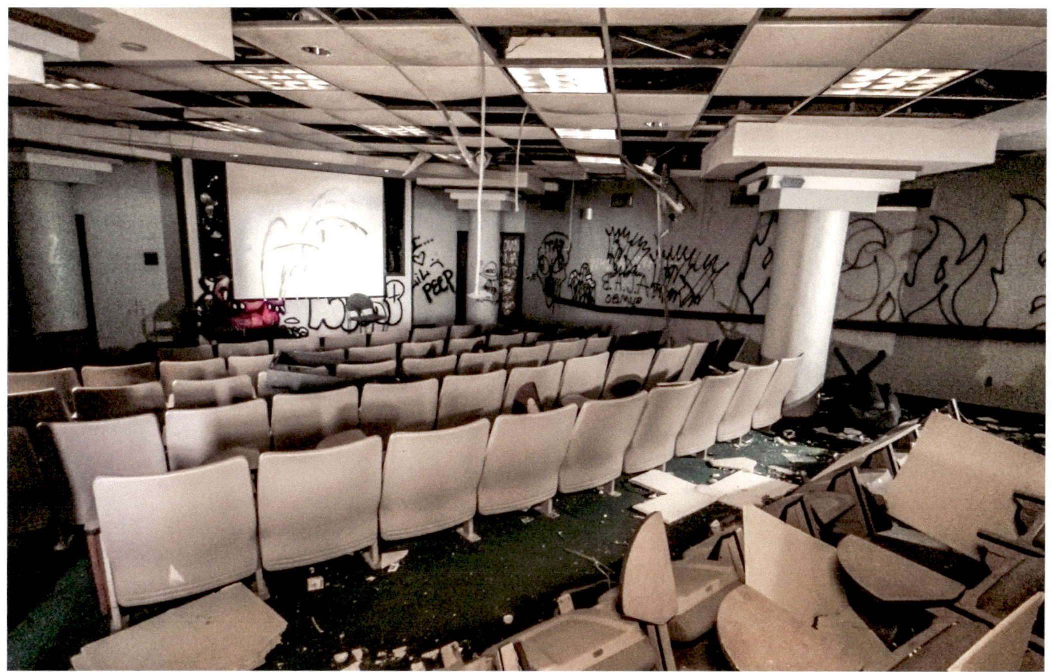

This old theater inside one of the buildings still has rows of seats facing the empty projector screen. The krewe had been searching for this room over the many times we explored the complex. We were thankful to finally find it on our final visit, though the room had been taken over by graffiti and scattered debris.

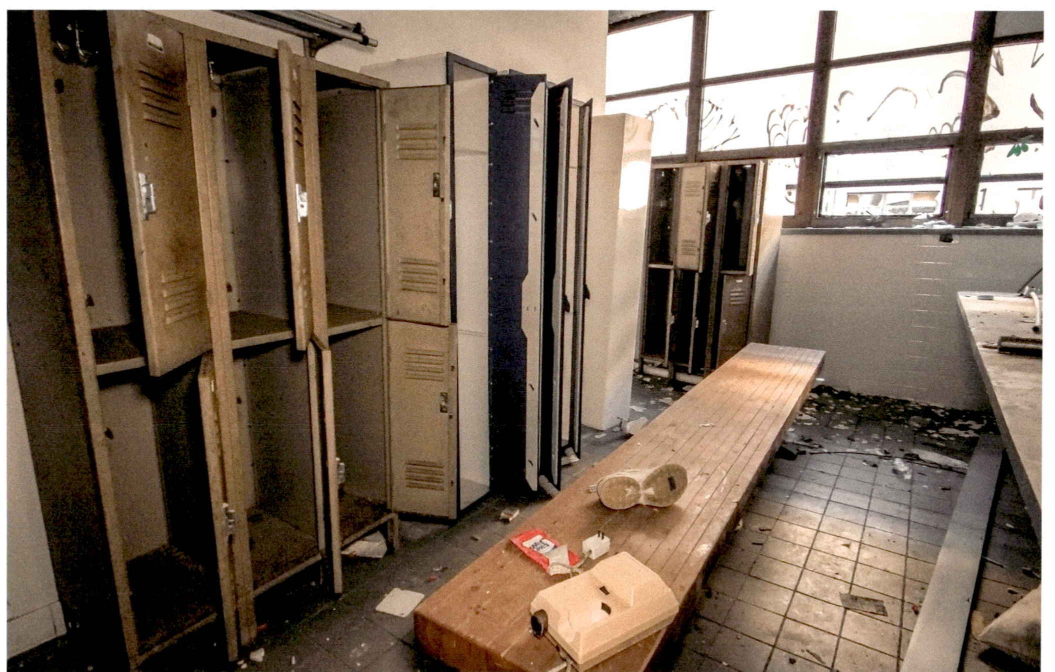

In another building, we found a locker room inside a gym. Now, it is just a forgotten space where personnel once changed for their workout or back to a uniform for work.

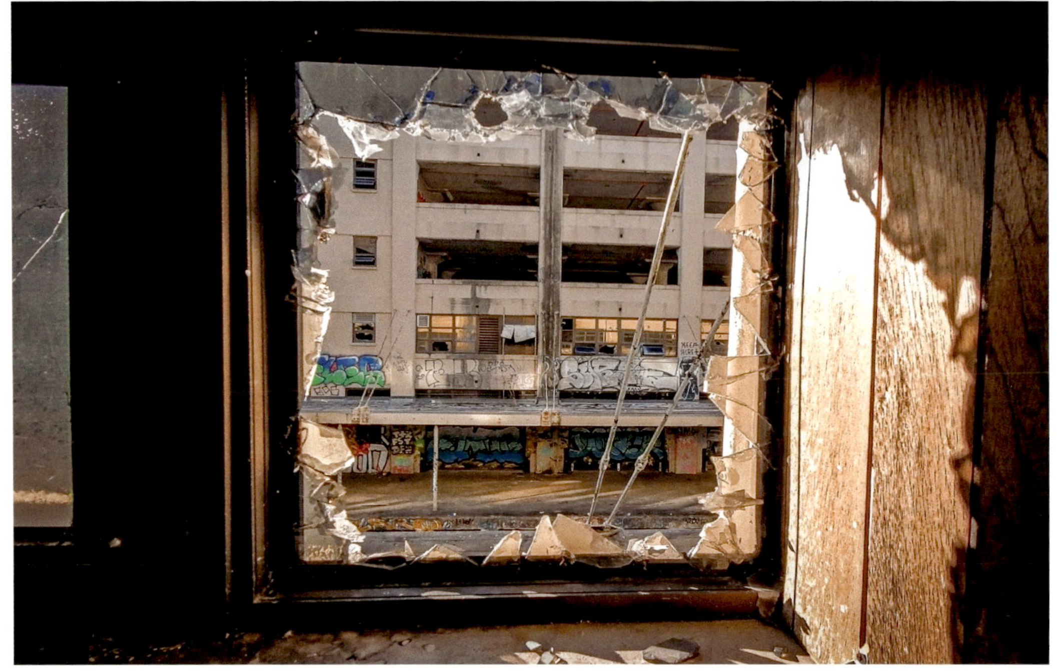

A shattered window frame offers a glimpse from one building to another. The broken glass edges reflect the late afternoon light, emphasizing the contrast between the building's interior shadows and the bright, graffiti-covered building beyond.

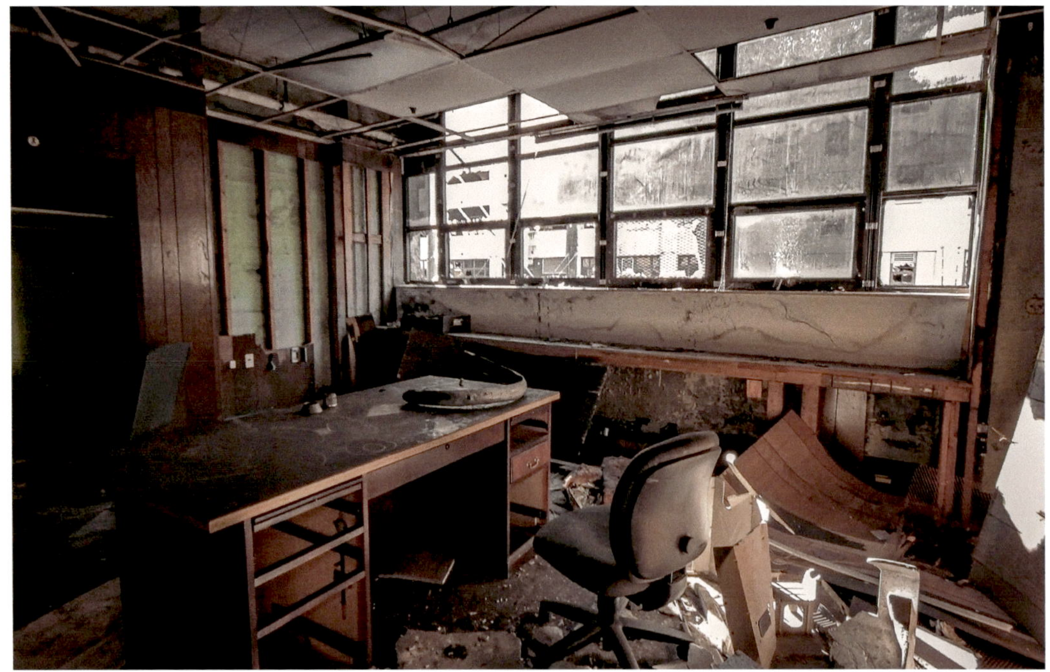

An office space where its desk and chairs still remain. The size of the office indicates it was more than likely used by a high-ranking officer.

5

NEW ORLEANS CIVIL DEFENSE COMMAND CENTER

A Cold War Relic Beneath the Floodwaters

The New Orleans Civil Defense Command Center, a significant but often overlooked structure, once played a unique role in the city's history. Originally conceived during the Cold War era, the bunker's purpose and use evolved over time, reflecting changes in both military strategy and local needs.

Research from the website New Orleans Historical, shows that the bunker was built in the 1950s. It was designed as a secure, fortified facility for government officials and emergency personnel to coordinate operations during a nuclear attack. It was a critical component of the city's emergency infrastructure, which included more than seventy strategically placed air-raid sirens. Engineered to shield occupants from radiation and blast effects, the bunker ensured the continuity of government functions and emergency response efforts during a crisis.

The two-story bunker had every necessity to aid its occupants. On the first floor was a communications center, offices for the mayor and staff, and a mechanical room with generators to keep the facilities running. In the center was a huge room used for strategic command decision-making. The second floor featured a common gathering room at its center, an infirmary with two medical beds, a kitchen and mess area, offices, and a large sleeping quarters with many bunk beds.

However, as the Cold War waned and the immediate threat of nuclear conflict diminished, the role of the bunker began to shift. It was repurposed for various functions, including as a headquarters for storm emergency operations.

In the mid-1990s, the bunker was decommissioned and deserted. Advances in technology and changes in emergency management practices rendered the old bunker irrelevant. The decision to close the facility was influenced by factors such as the high cost of maintenance, outdated infrastructure, and the availability of more modern facilities better suited to contemporary needs.

The facility remained unused and began to deteriorate. In the years following, it experienced significant issues with flooding. The facility's location and aging infrastructure made it vulnerable to water intrusion, exacerbated by heavy rains and the broader challenges of New Orleans' drainage system.

The first floor has been largely submerged since its closure, with water damage contributing to its ongoing deterioration. The flooding has persisted for years, leaving the facility inaccessible with several feet of water mixed with oil and diesel fuel sitting stagnant for over thirty years.

When the chance to explore this bunker came up, we did not hesitate. The krewe quickly stocked up on rubber waders and respirator masks to protect ourselves from the hazards we knew awaited us. Over two separate visits, we ventured deep underground, armed only with our cameras, flashlights, and a sense of adventure. The pitch-black corridors of the first floor were still partially flooded, with the nasty water reaching up to our hips as we moved cautiously through the space.

Beneath the brown liquid, our boots met all sorts of strange, unidentifiable objects, each step carrying the risk of finding an unseen hole or becoming snagged on something that might trap us. The air was thick with the overpowering smells of diesel, oil, mold, and mildew, making it one of the most uninviting places we had ever encountered. Yet, despite the challenges, we were determined to document every corner of this hidden underground world.

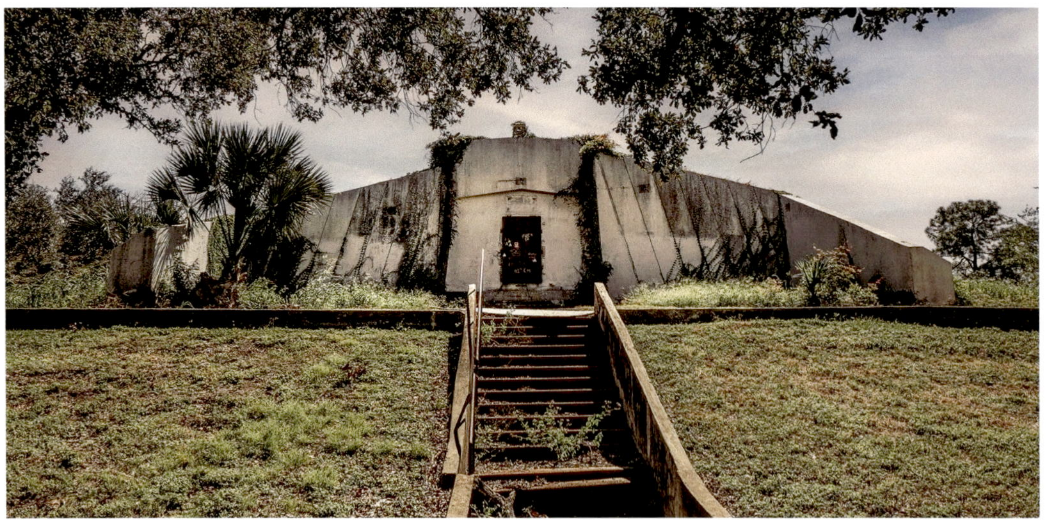

The New Orleans Civil Defense Command Center, built in the 1950s, served as an emergency command post during the Cold War. Located near Lake Pontchartrain, it was designed to protect officials in case of nuclear attack but was eventually used as a hurricane command center before it was deserted in the mid-1990s.

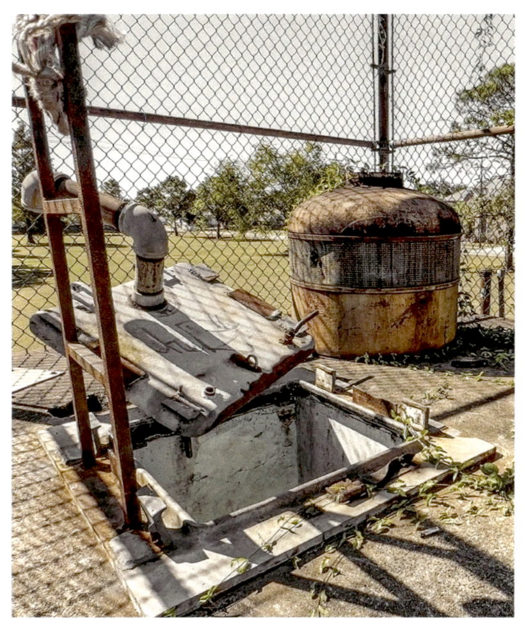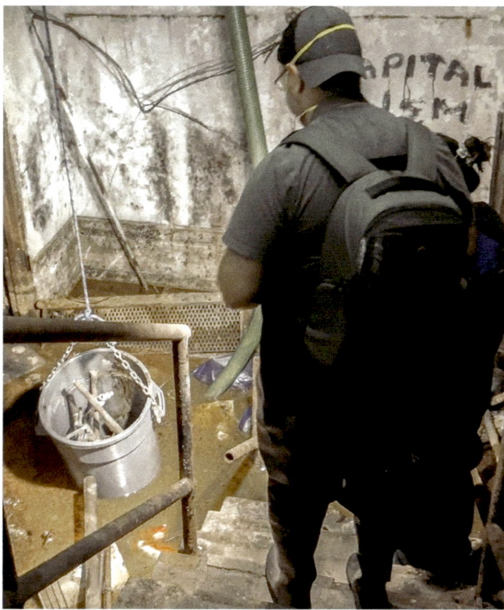

Above left: Atop a grassy hill in the middle of the neutral ground, the rusted vent shafts and escape hatch of the bunker rise above ground, revealing part of its hidden infrastructure. Designed to provide ventilation and a secure exit, these structures are the few visible remnants of the bunker from the outside.

Above right: Descending far down to the entrance of the bunker, the krewe were met with nearly 4 feet of stagnant water, a mix of diesel fuel, oil, and decades-old debris. The murky liquid, left undisturbed for over thirty years, filled the confined space with an acrid smell, adding to the dangerous conditions.

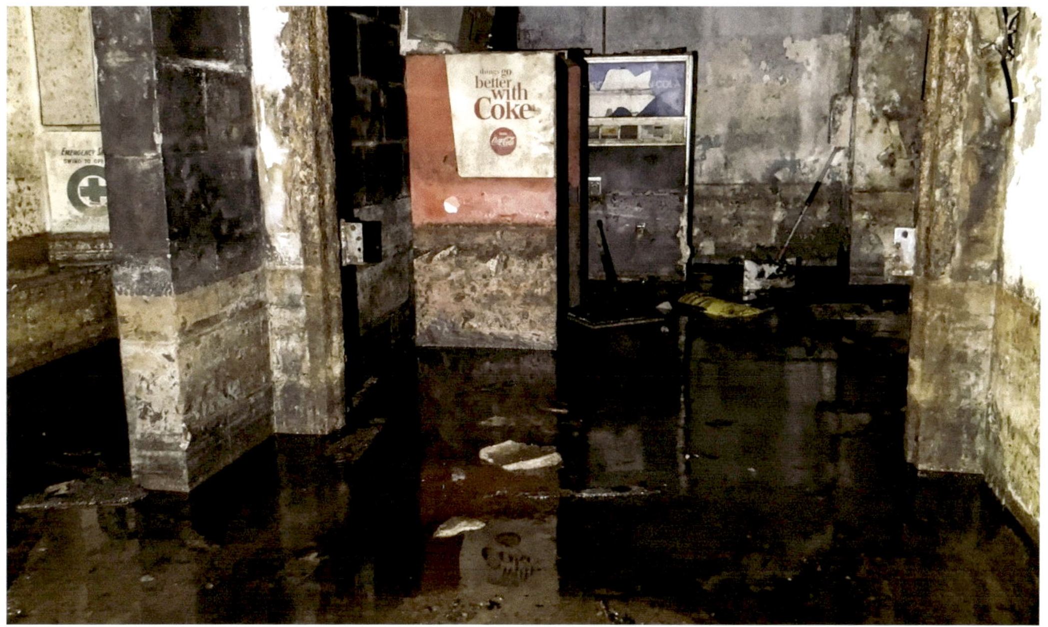

Inside the flooded bunker, a pair of vintage soda machines sit submerged, their faded logos a reminder of a different time. The nasty still water reflects the light from our flashlights, while rust and grime have overtaken every surface.

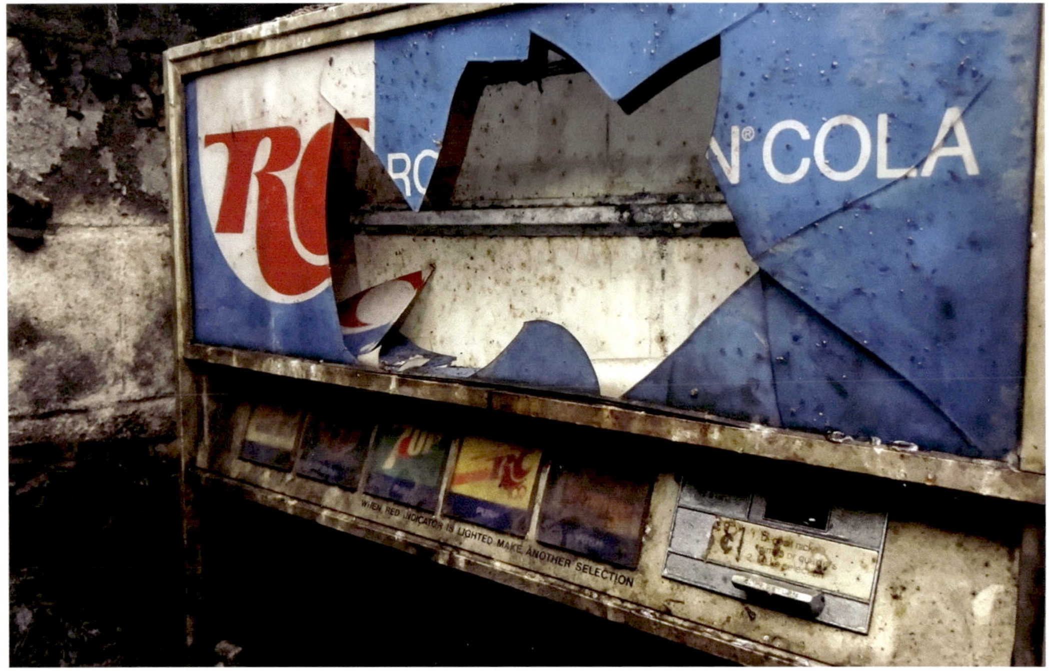

One of the soda machines is an old RC Cola vending machine. It still sits in the nasty water broken and forgotten. The faded colors and shattered plastic reveal decades of neglect, a relic of a time when cold sodas were a small comfort in the underground shelter. We were unable to open it to see if any bottles were still left inside.

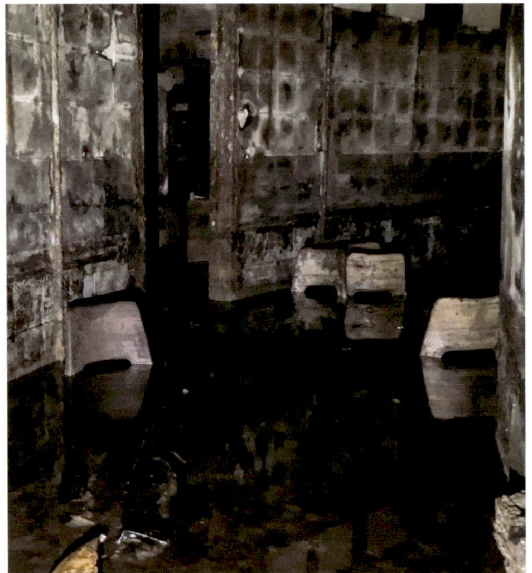

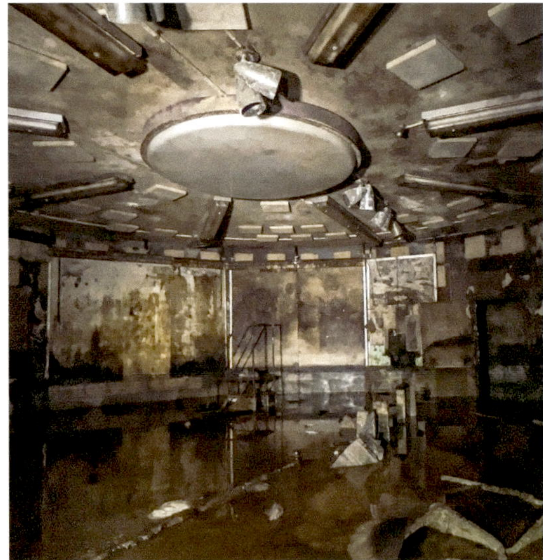

Above left: Navigating the dark, flooded corridors of the first floor was not easy. The walls were covered in peeling paint and blackened grime, while old chairs sat partially submerged. Each step we took had to be slow and cautious as we had no idea what we were stepping on or in.

Above right: In the center of the first floor was a large circular room that was still partially submerged. This was the main briefing room for the bunker. First as a military fallout shelter, and then eventually as a hurricane command center for the city's top officials.

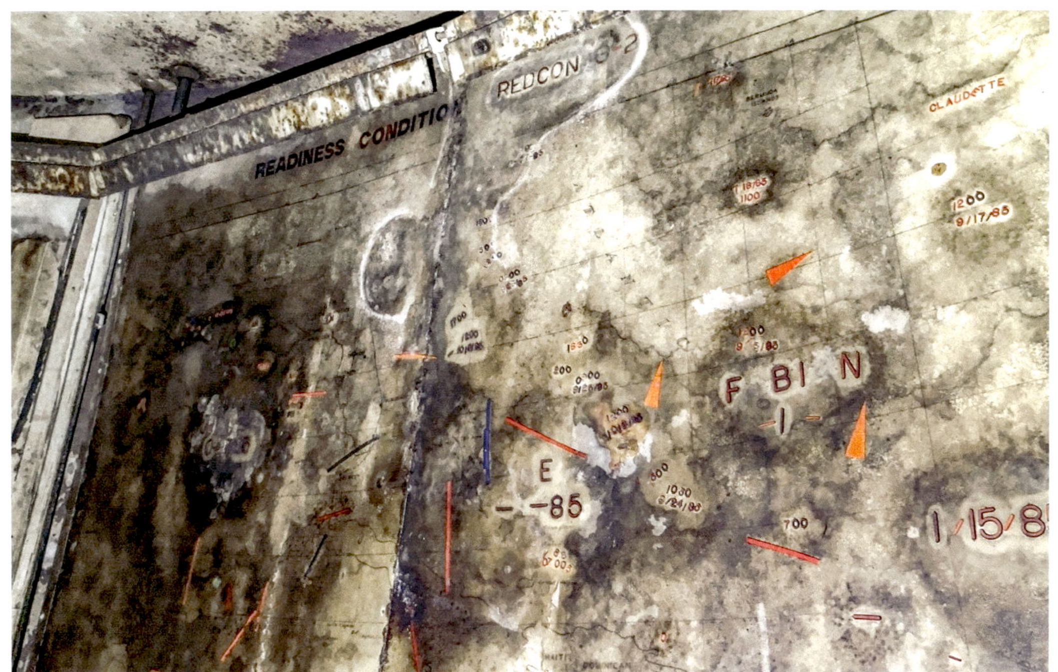

In the large briefing room, a weathered wall map in the command center displayed faded markings and readiness conditions, labeled "READINESS CONDITION/REDCON G-2." The annotations and dates, such as "Claudette," "Fabian," and entries from the 1980s, reveal its use in tracking tropical storms and hurricanes.

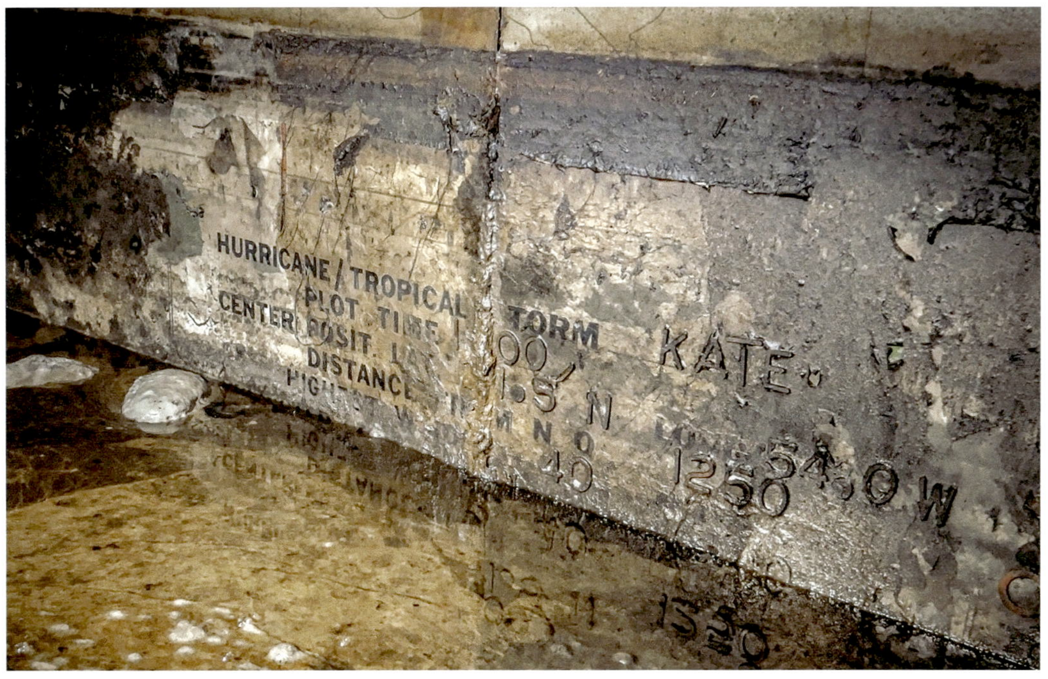

A faded and grimy wall inscription at the bottom of the map details the coordinates and tracking data for Hurricane Kate which took place in November 1985.

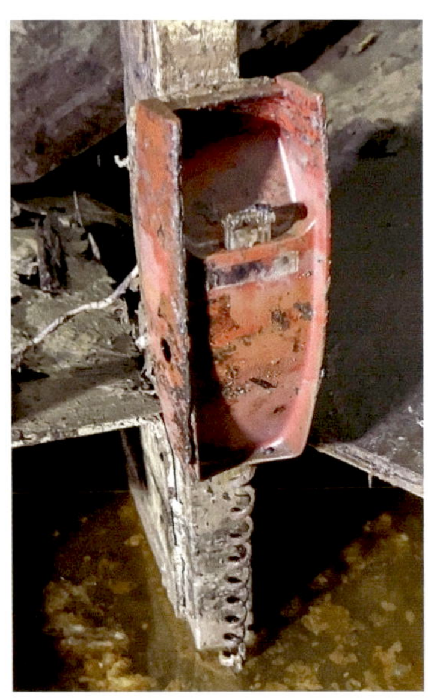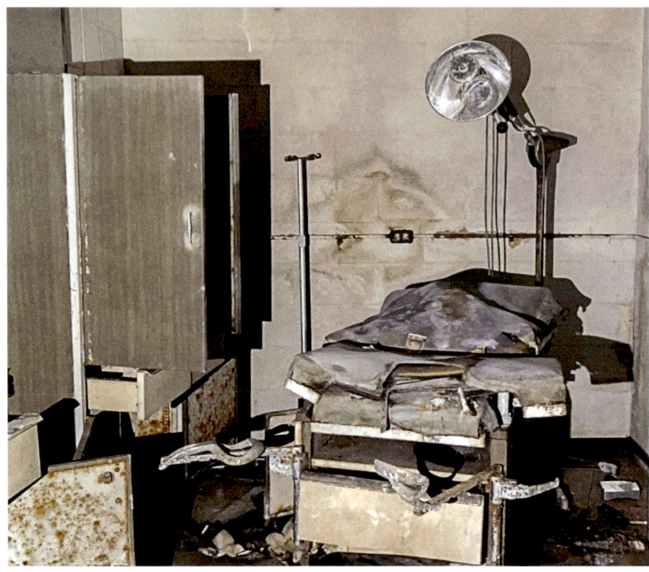

Above left: An old emergency phone, with its faded red casing, still hangs on a corroded support beam in what we believe was the communication center. The phone cord for the handset led into the nasty water, and I made the decision not to try and fish it out.

Above right: On the second floor, we discovered an old infirmary with an examination table. The overhead light for the table, now rusted, still hangs above.

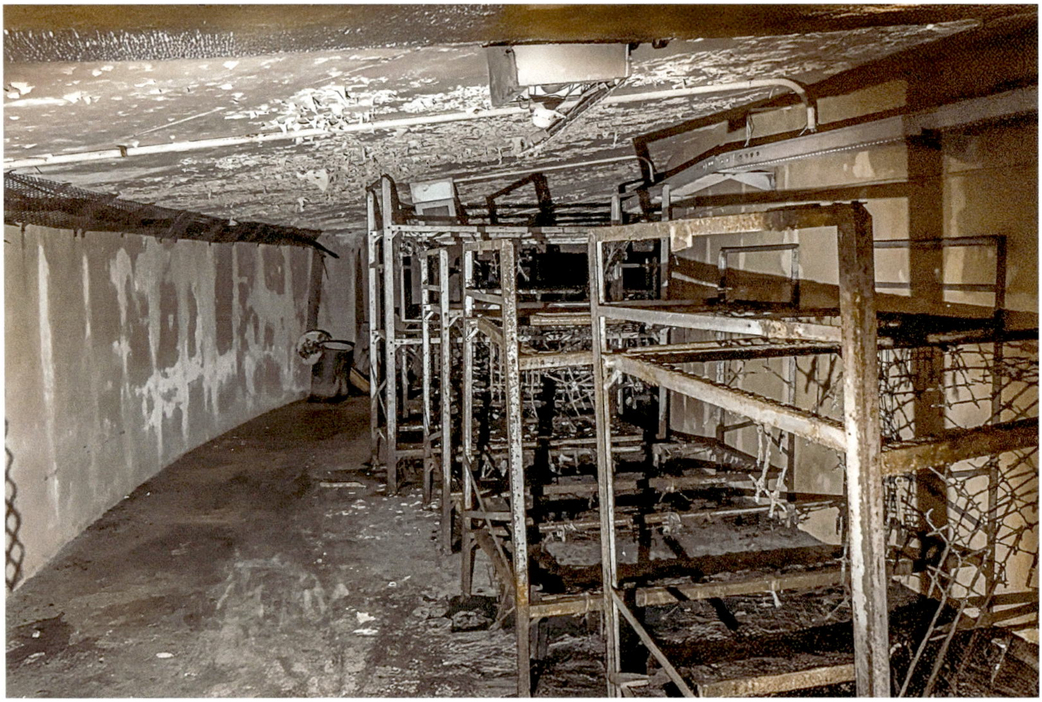

Also on the second floor, in the outermost corridor, we found rows of rusted metal bunk beds that lined the cramped curved quarters of the wall. Their sagging springs and broken frames show decades of decay.

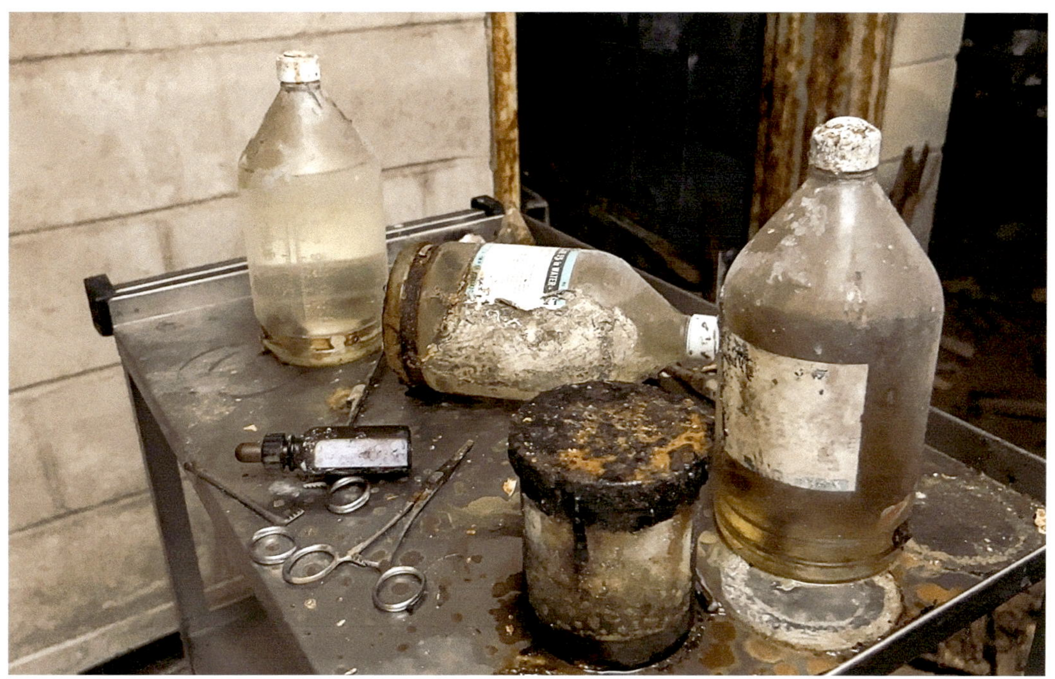

In the infirmary, we found a rusted metal cart with some surgical scissors and old glass bottles filled with unknown liquid.

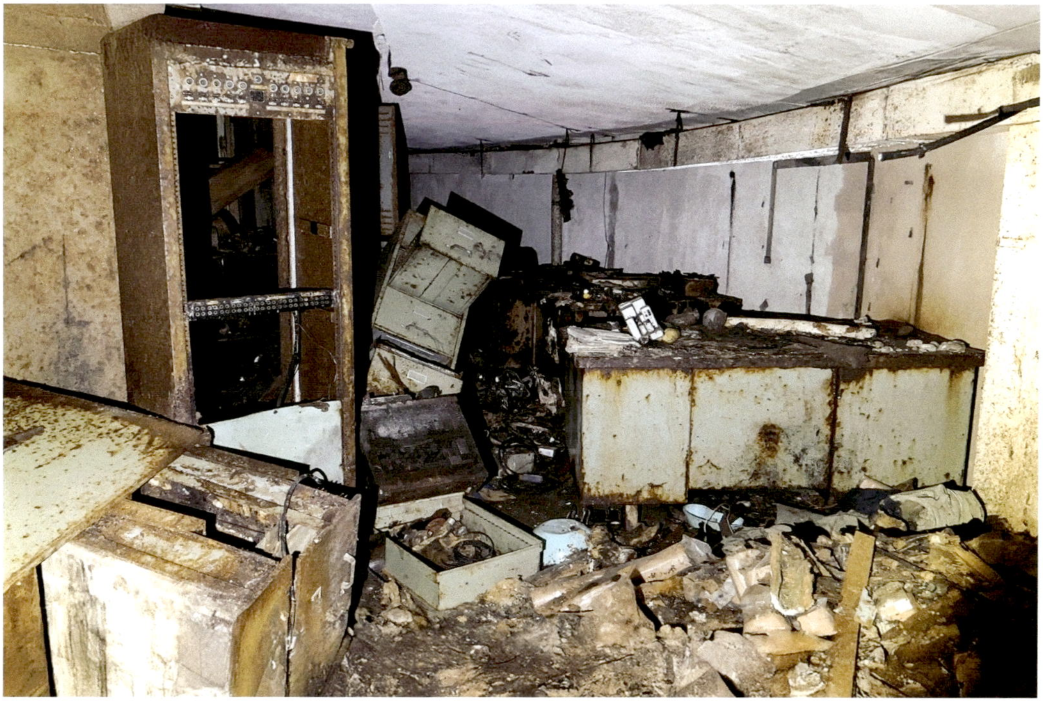

Inside one of the offices on the second floor reveals toppled file cabinets, broken equipment, and piles of debris scattered across the floor. The corroded metal and collapsed shelving tell a story of either vandals looking for scrap to steal or just time taking its toll on everything.

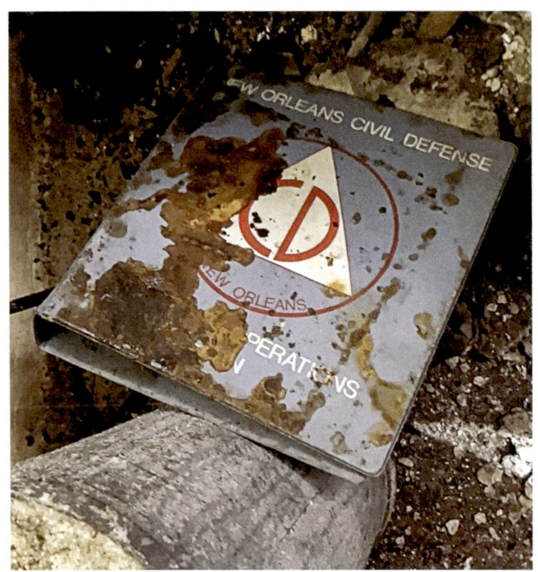 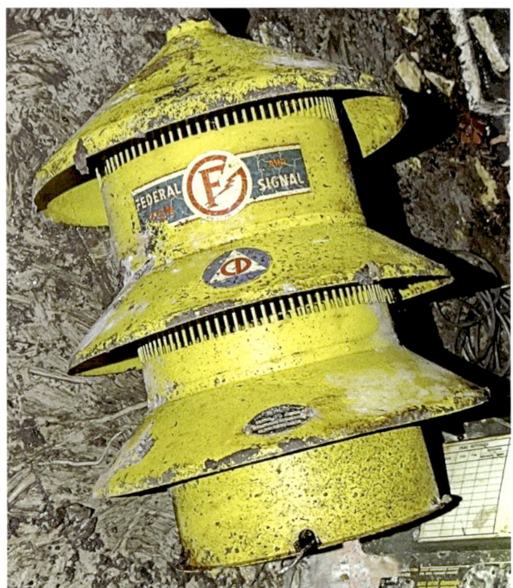

Above left: An old operations manual from the New Orleans Civil Defense lies forgotten on the floor. The worn logo serves as a reminder of the shelter's role during tense times, when detailed planning and readiness were essential.

Above right: An old Federal Signal air raid siren housing rests on the floor. The siren itself is long gone. It was one of the over seventy sirens placed around New Orleans to alert residents of impending threats.

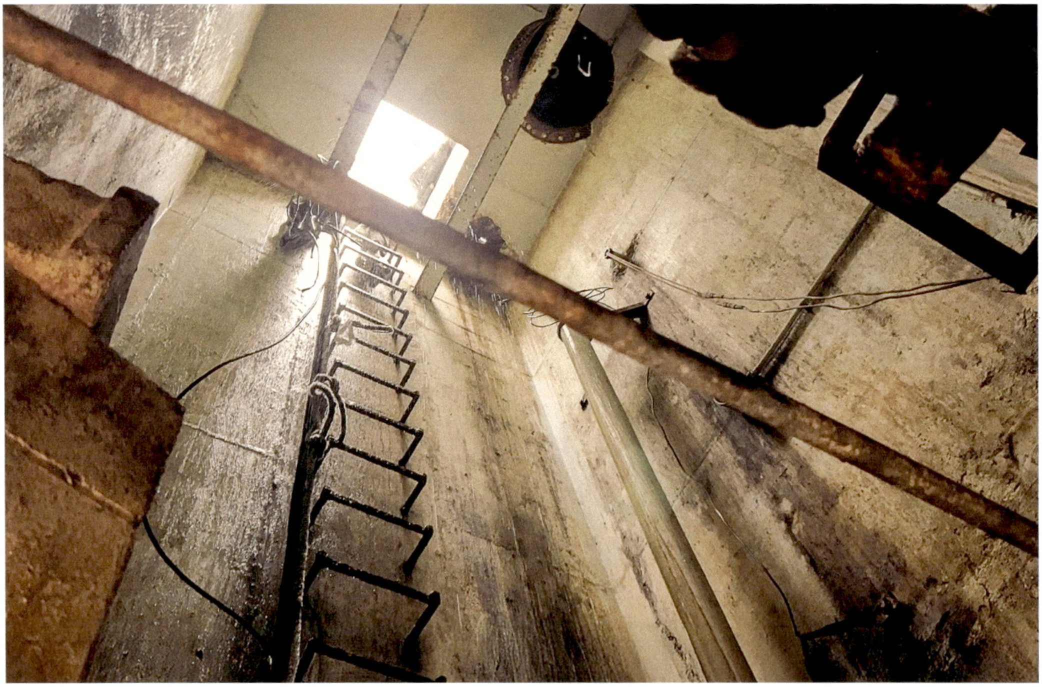

Back down on the first floor, we slowly made our way through the flooded equipment room to find the other end of the escape hatch we saw from outside. After many twists and turns, we located it. The view from below the escape hatch shows rusted metal rungs that lead up the concrete shaft to the surface. This hidden passage served as a critical emergency exit for occupants of the bunker.

6

DEGAULLE MANOR AND EXHIBITBE

From Housing Complex to Cultural Canvas

Information on Alchetron.com indicates that Degaulle Manor was built in 1964 and originally named Bridge Plaza. Over 400 units were available for families to move into. However, by the 1970s, the complex became Section-8 Housing for low-income families and would have a long history of mismanagement.

Over the years, the combination of poor management, underfunding, and lack of adequate maintenance caused the property to fall into disrepair. The buildings began to deteriorate, with basic infrastructure issues like faulty plumbing, broken windows, and roof leaks becoming commonplace. Residents frequently dealt with unsafe living conditions, rat infestations, and broken elevators.

Throughout the 1980s and 1990s, it had developed a reputation for rampant crime. Drug deals, shootings, and gang activity were commonplace, with law enforcement often reluctant or refusing to help. Over the years, more and more families moved out or were evicted and the population of the complex dwindled. In 2012, the few remaining tenants were evicted from the property, and it has been deserted ever since.

In 2014, the site found an unexpected new purpose. New Orleans artist Brandan "BMike" Odums transformed the vacant buildings into an art exhibit called *ExhibitBE*, which became one of the largest street art installations in the South. Over the course of several months, local and visiting artists covered the exterior and interior walls of the deserted complex with striking murals and graffiti art, using the space to explore themes of racial injustice and cultural pride. The artwork featured powerful images of civil rights leaders, community figures, and bold depictions of black life in New Orleans.

ExhibitBE quickly became a cultural phenomenon, drawing thousands of visitors from across the country. For a brief time, the forgotten ruins were revitalized, not as a place of despair but as a vibrant canvas for hope, healing, and social commentary. Though the exhibit was temporary, closing after only a few months, it left a lasting impression on those who experienced it. Today, the remnants still stand, though they are slowly succumbing to the elements.

We were fully aware of the dangers this site posed, but that did not keep us away. When the krewe arrived, a light rain had just started to fall. From the outside, we could already see what was left of the art installation, but we had no idea of the incredible artwork waiting for us inside some of the units.

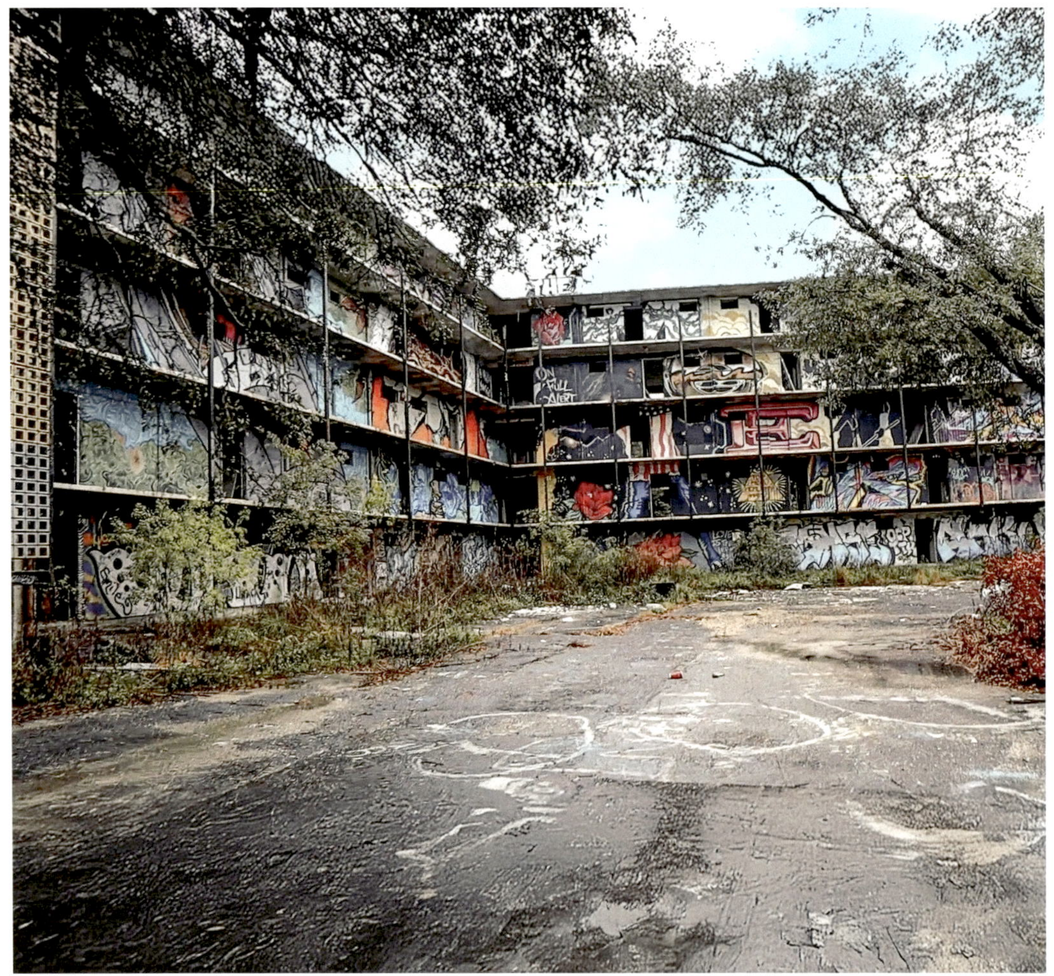

Degaulle Manor, a 450-unit housing complex, first opened in 1964 and has been deserted since 2012. However, in 2014, local artist Brandan "BMike" Odums, along with other artists, transformed it into an art installation called *ExhibitBE*, adorning the walls with powerful murals of civil rights leaders and other prominent figures of color.

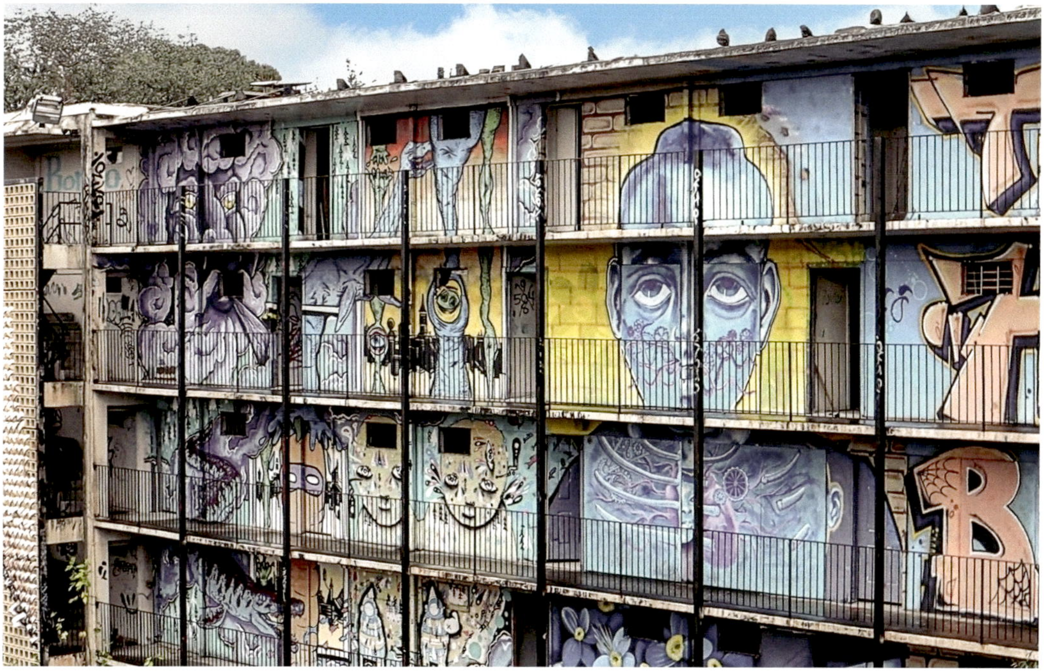

Colorful murals now cover every surface of this deserted apartment complex, transforming its walls into a powerful visual statement. The vibrant artwork contrasts with the building's decay, creating an unexpected blend of art and neglect.

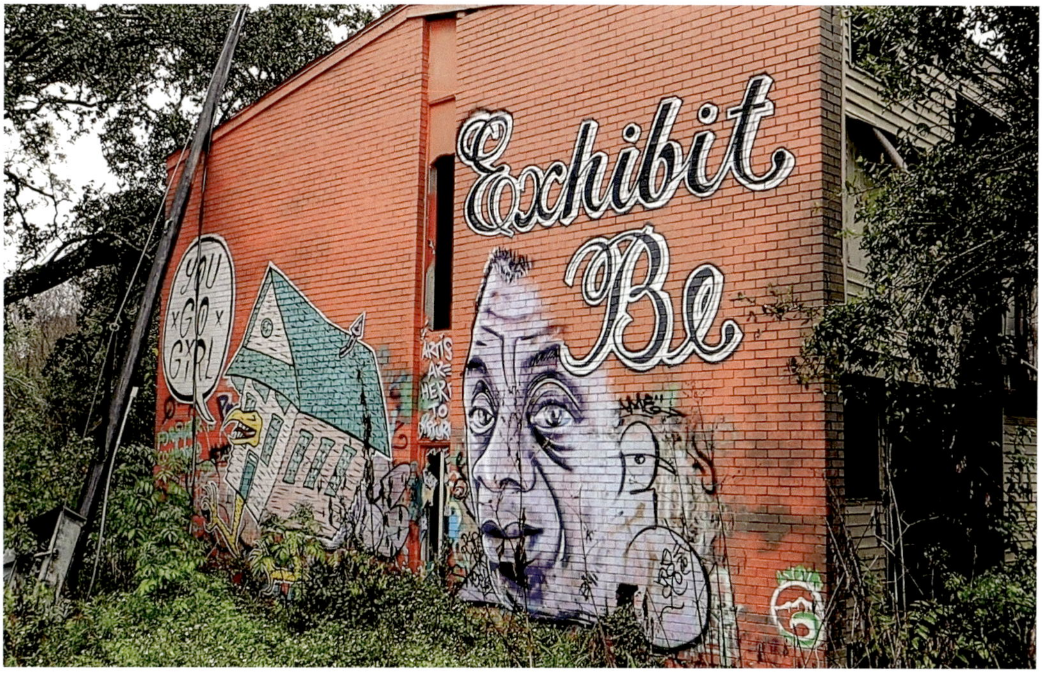

The complex became a vibrant canvas where artists covered walls with large-scale portraits and messages.

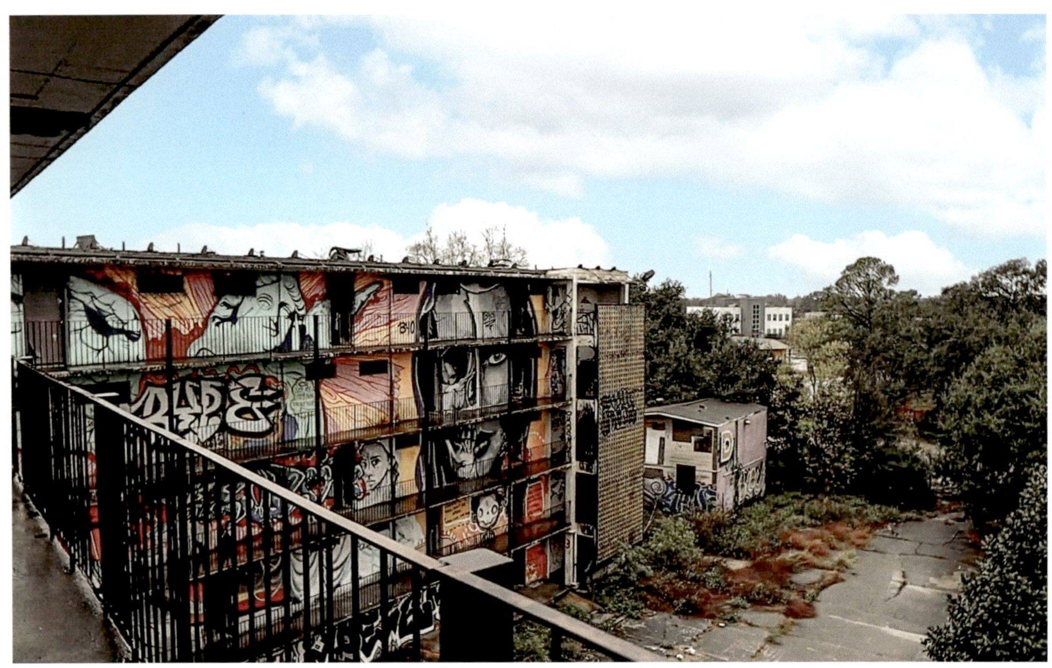

The upper floors offer a striking view of the once-bustling apartment units now overtaken by vibrant murals. Now it is just left to the elements.

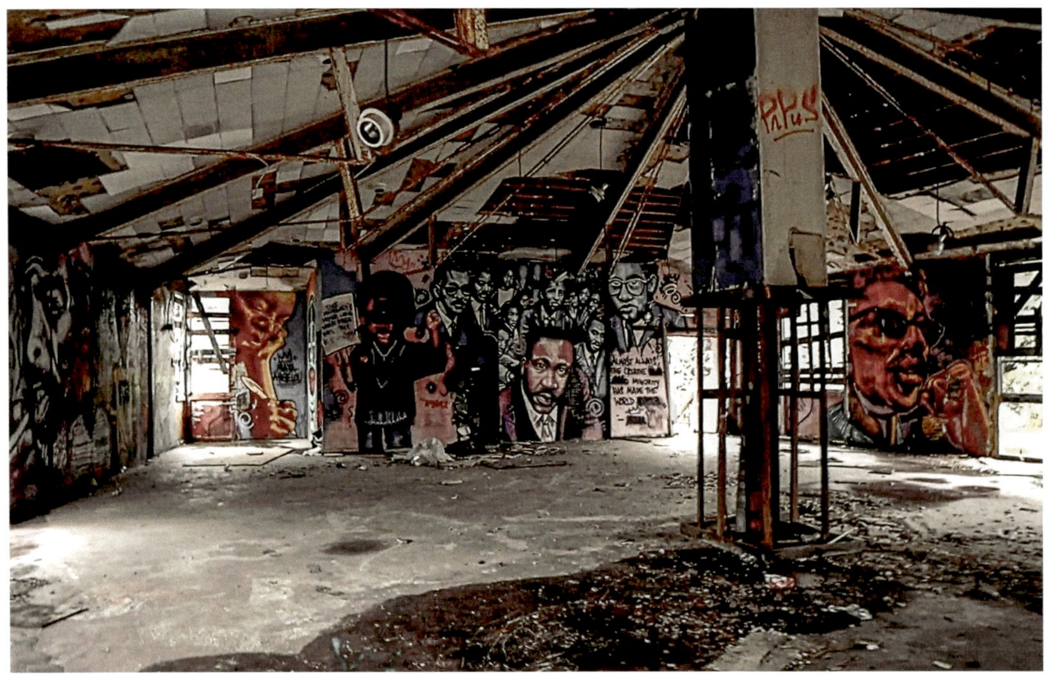

Despite the former recreation center's desertion, the vivid expressions on its walls reflect the enduring spirit of creativity and resilience.

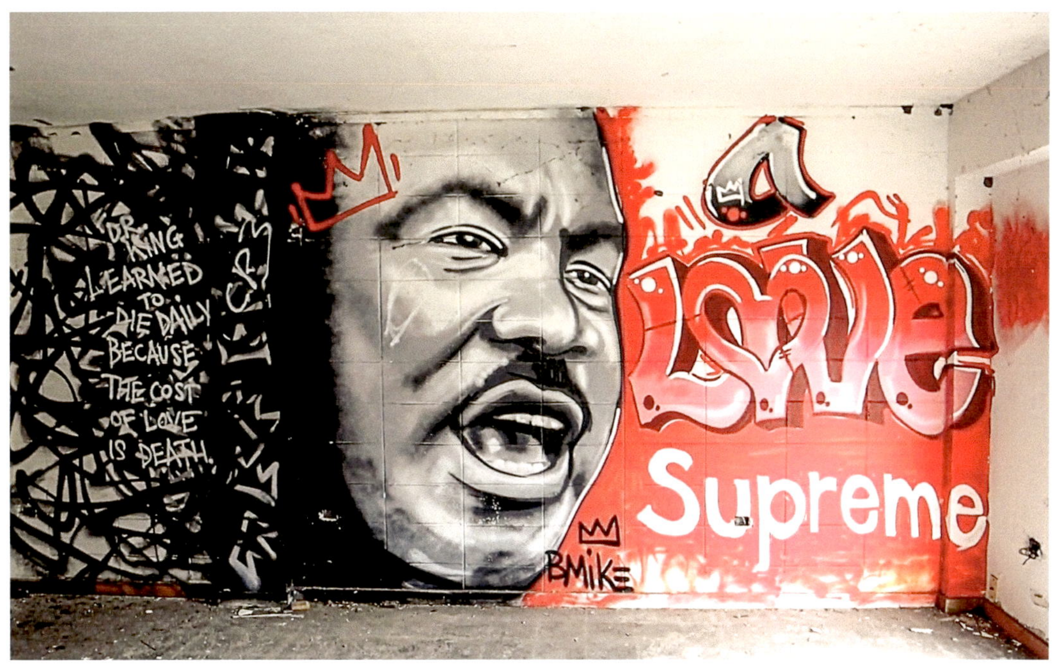

A powerful mural of Dr. Martin Luther King, Jr. graces the walls of one of the old units and bears the words "A Love Supreme" emblazoned in vibrant red. This striking artwork by "BMike" pays homage to King's legacy, turning this space into a gallery for voices that inspire and provoke thought. The message serves as a reminder of the enduring fight for justice and the cost of love in the pursuit of equality.

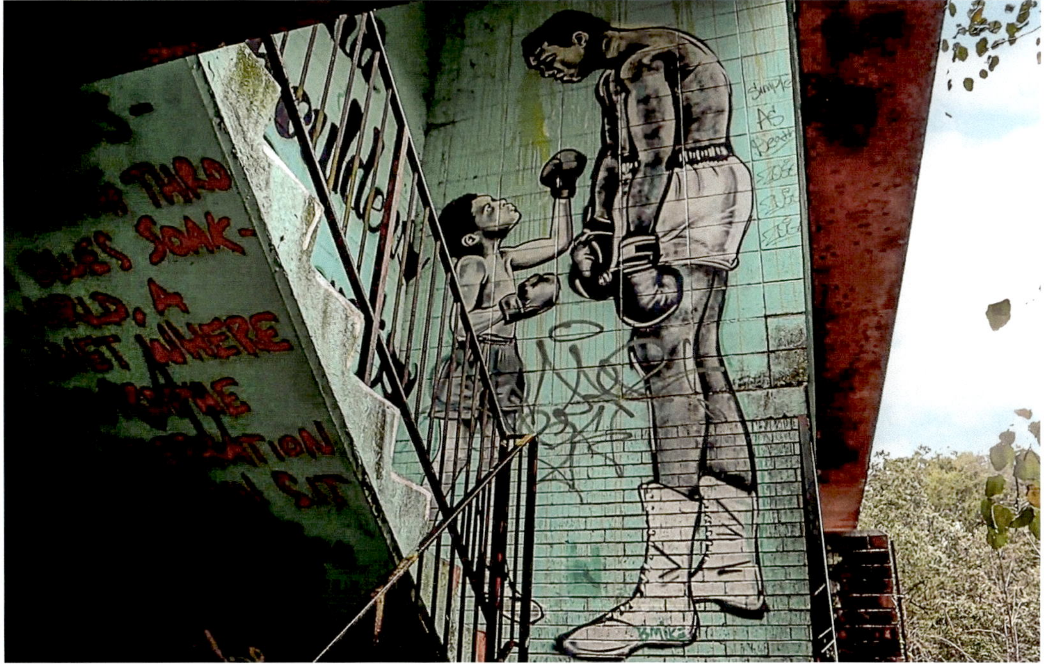

Muhammad Ali towers over a young child on a stairwell wall, capturing a moment of connection between generations.

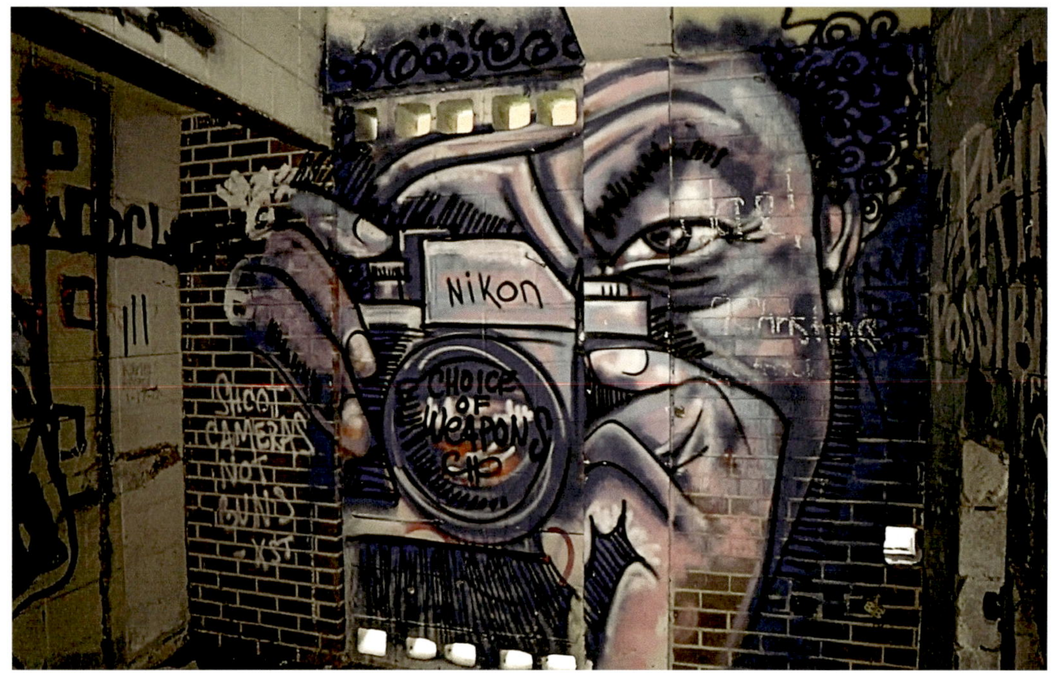

This mural features a photographer holding a camera; the words "Choice of Weapons" reflecting a message of non-violence. Tucked away in one of the corridors, it challenges viewers to shoot with cameras, not guns, turning the decayed surroundings into a call for change and creative expression.

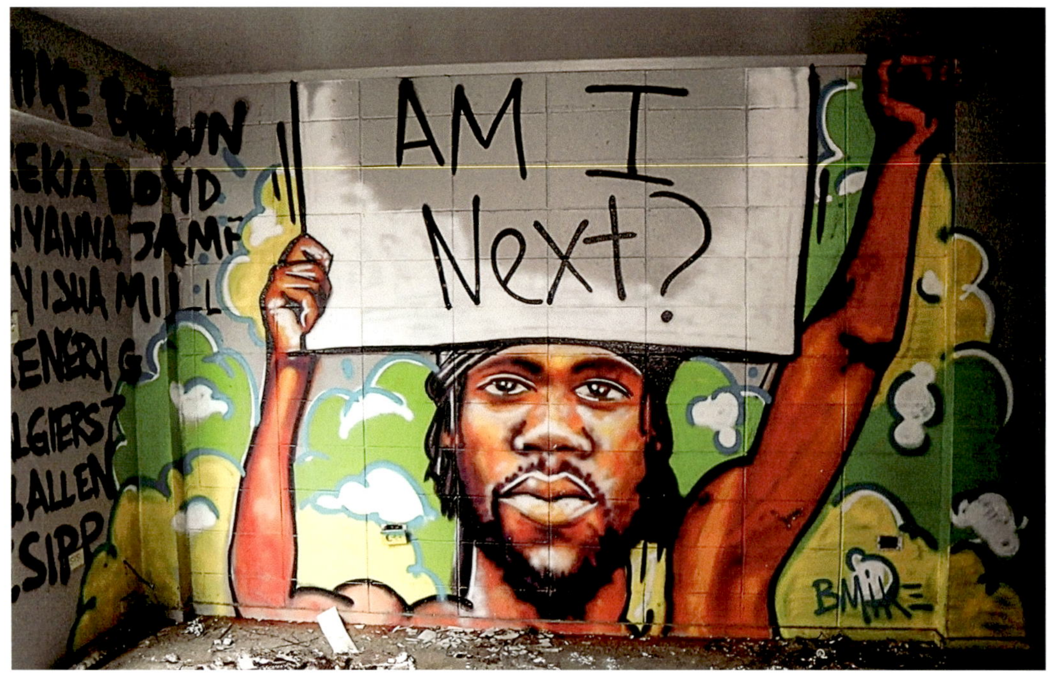

This powerful image captures the ongoing struggle against injustice, asking the haunting question, "Am I Next?".

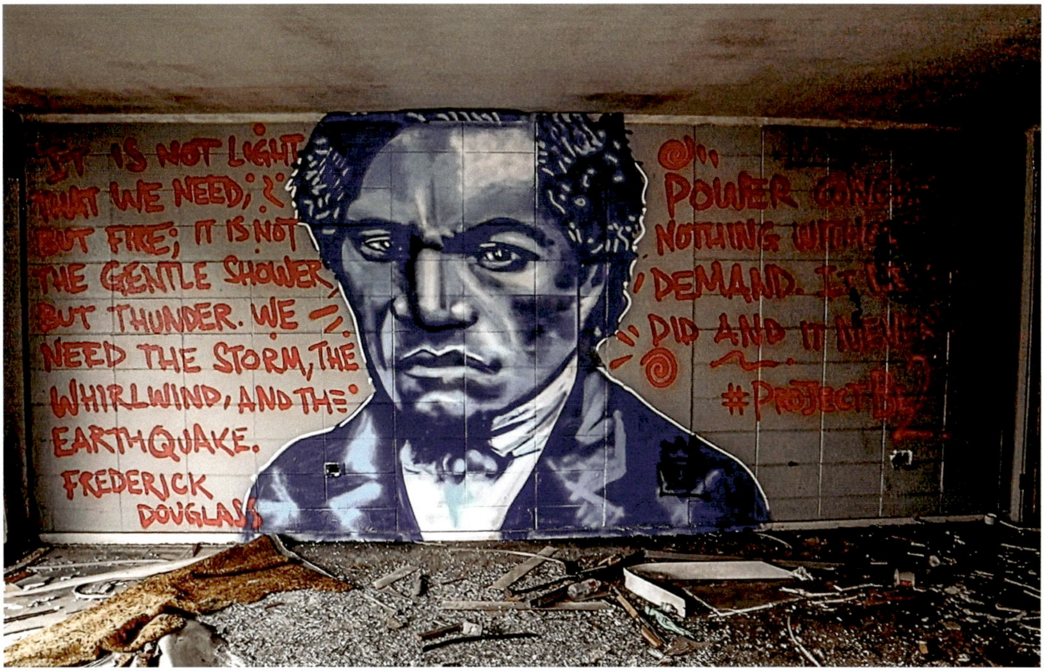

An image of Frederick Douglass stares boldly from the wall, framed by his own powerful words from his famous speech from July 5, 1852: "It is not light that we need, but fire; it is not the gentle shower, but thunder. We need the storm, the whirlwind, and the earthquake."

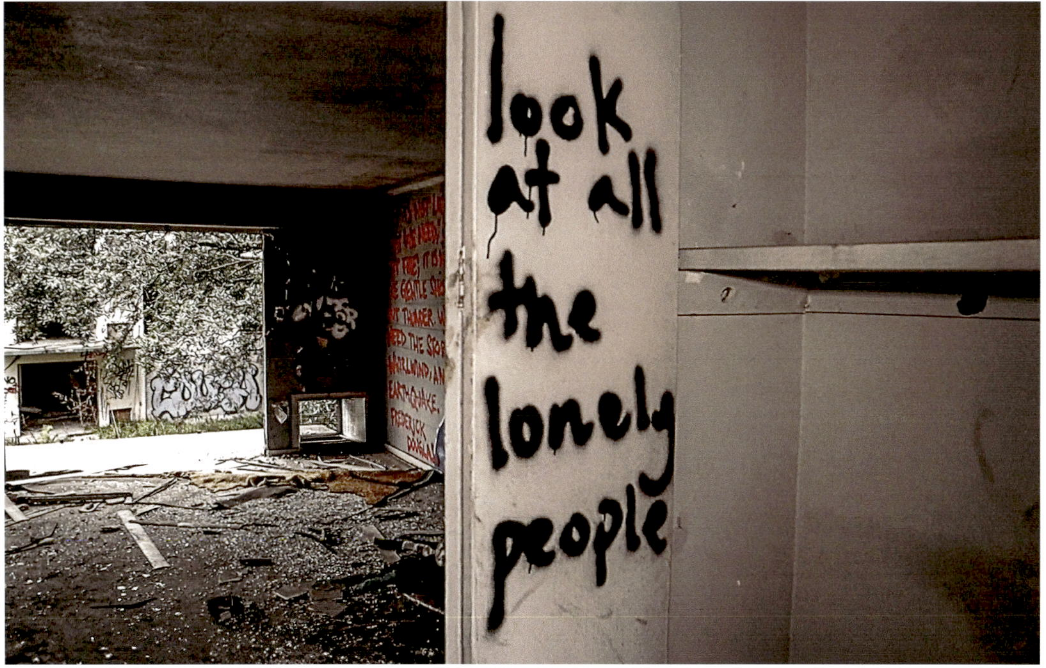

A simple message scrawled on the wall reads, "look at all the lonely people." The words echo through the vacant hallways, capturing a sense of abandonment and forgotten lives that once filled this space. Now, the silence speaks louder than ever.

7

HOLY CROSS SCHOOL

A Legacy of Education, Desertion, and Uncertain Futures

The Holy Cross School's website explains that in 1859, a plantation on the Mississippi River was purchased by the Congregation of Holy Cross (formed in 1837). It goes on to say that the plantation's property, known as Reynes Farm, would be used for a boarding school named Saint Isidore's College. Then in 1895, the administration building was opened, and the school was renamed to Holy Cross School.

In 1912, a new wing on either side of the building was added completing the structure as it still stands today. Throughout the twentieth century, Holy Cross School continued to flourish, becoming an integral part of the Lower Ninth Ward community. The school's students formed lifelong bonds on its campus, and the school became a source of pride for the neighborhood. The Holy Cross Tigers, the name of the school's athletic teams, were particularly renowned, drawing large crowds to their games and fostering a strong sense of community spirit.

The school also played a significant role in shaping the cultural and social fabric of the Lower Ninth Ward. Generations of families sent their sons to Holy Cross, and the school became a symbol of hope and opportunity for many. Many alumni went on to achieve success in various fields, including business, politics, and the arts, further cementing the school's legacy as a pillar of the community.

The turning point for the school came in August 2005, when Hurricane Katrina arrived. The Lower Ninth Ward was one of the hardest-hit areas, and the campus was submerged under several feet of water. The damage was catastrophic not only to the school, but to the entire neighborhood surrounding it.

In the wake of the disaster, the school's leadership faced an impossible decision. The cost of rebuilding was astronomical, and the future of the neighborhood was uncertain. Ultimately, the decision was made to relocate the school to a new site in Gentilly, a neighborhood on higher ground. In 2007, after more than a century in its original location, Holy Cross School officially moved, leaving behind its historic campus.

Since the relocation, the old campus has remained deserted, its once-grand building slowly deteriorating. Windows are shattered, doors hang off their hinges, and vegetation has overtaken the property.

The fate of the school has been the subject of much debate and controversy in New Orleans. Various proposals have been put forward to redevelop the site, ranging from housing projects to community centers. However, efforts to move forward have been hampered by disagreements over the best use of the land, concerns about preserving the historic building, and the ongoing challenges of revitalizing the neighborhood.

In recent years, there has been renewed interest in finding a solution that honors the legacy of Holy Cross School while addressing the needs of the current community. Some advocates have called for the preservation of the site as a historical landmark, while others argue for its redevelopment to provide much-needed resources and opportunities for the neighborhood. As of now, the future of the old campus remains uncertain, a blank slate awaiting its next chapter.

I had already seen photos of this school shared by other photographers on social media, but I was determined to capture the school with my own perspective. Stories of people falling through the second and third floors had circulated in the urban explorer community, so we approached the site with extreme caution, determined not to become part of those tales.

Despite our carefulness, one member of the krewe nearly fell through a weak spot in the floor. Thankfully, someone was close enough to grab his backpack, preventing what could have been a serious accident. Exploring deserted buildings always comes with risks, but the thrill of the adventure and the chance to document these places before they disappear forever often outweigh the dangers.

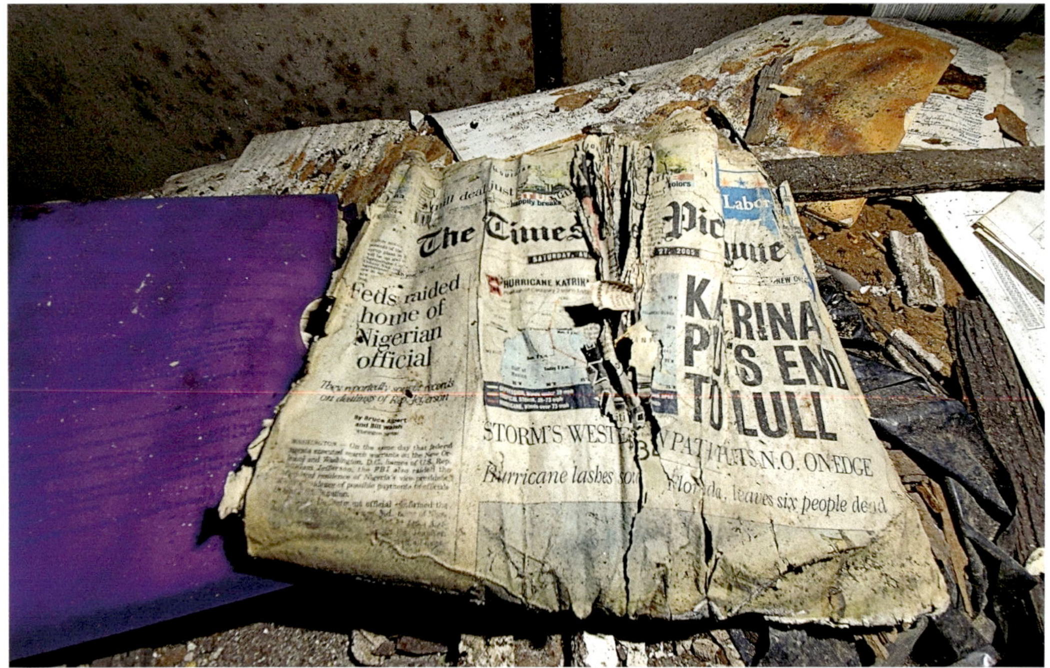

A tattered copy of The Times-Picayune newspaper, dated August 27, 2005, lies frozen in time from the eve of Hurricane Katrina's landfall. The faded headlines and brittle pages serve as a reminder of the day that changed New Orleans forever, now preserved in the ruins of Holy Cross.

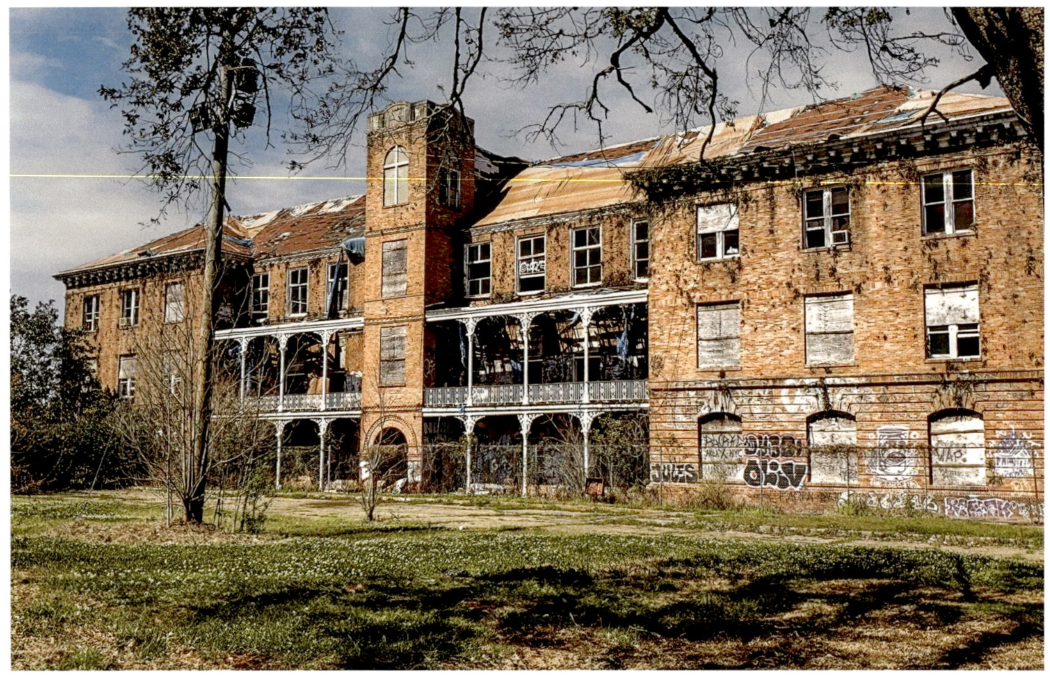

The former Holy Cross School served the Lower Ninth Ward for over a century. Deserted after it was devastated by Hurricane Katrina in 2005, the historic building now stands deteriorated and covered in graffiti.

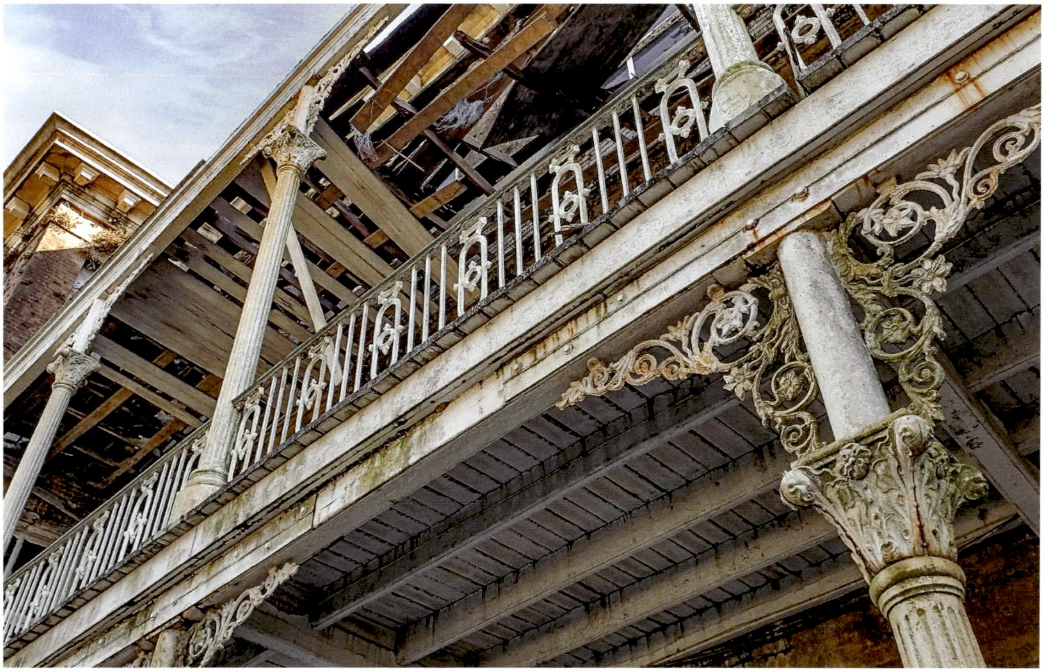

The ornate ironwork and weathered columns of the balcony, once symbols of architectural elegance, now show signs of decay, slowly eroding under the weight of time. These intricate details stand as a testament to the craftsmanship of the past.

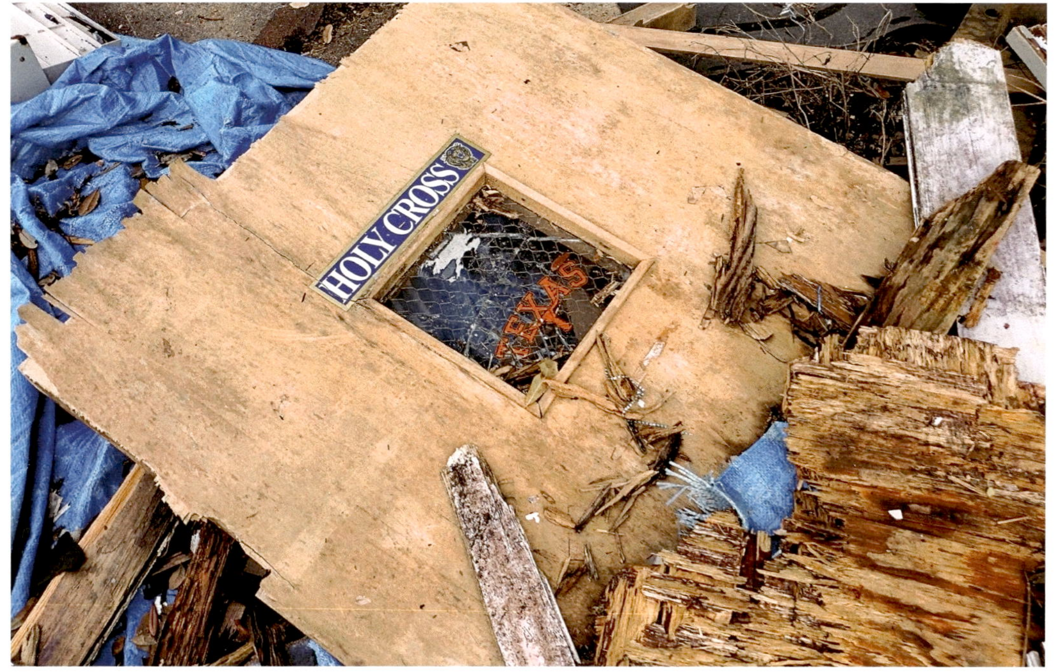

Amid the debris of the deserted school, a broken door emerges, bearing the institution's name.

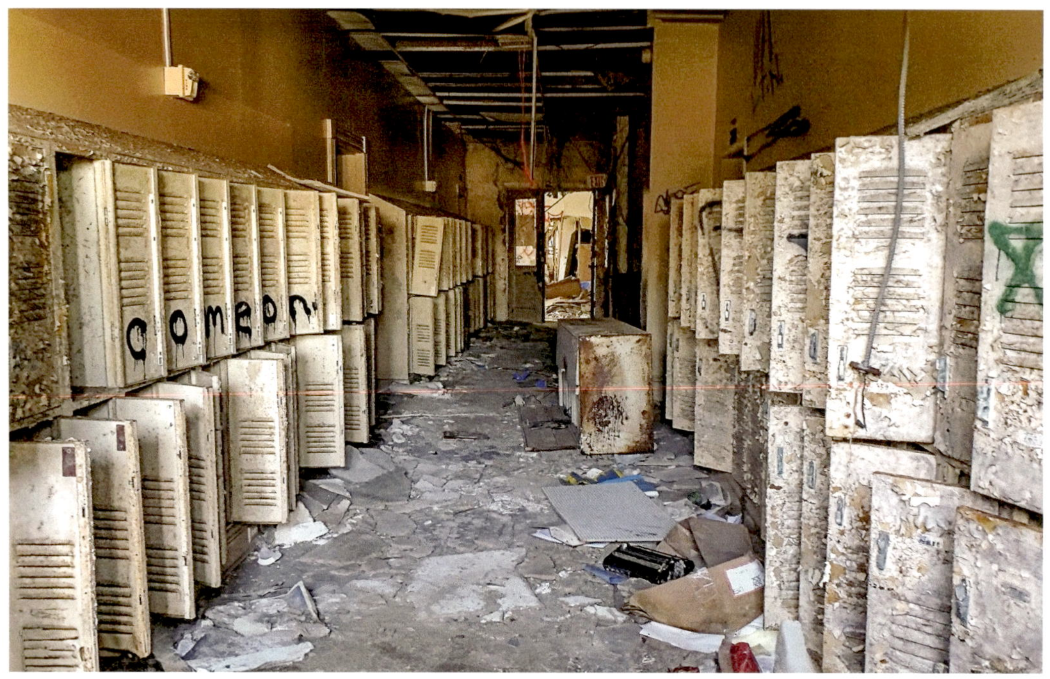

The hallways are now eerily silent, lined with rusted lockers and scattered debris. You can almost hear the hustle and bustle of the students opening and closing locker doors.

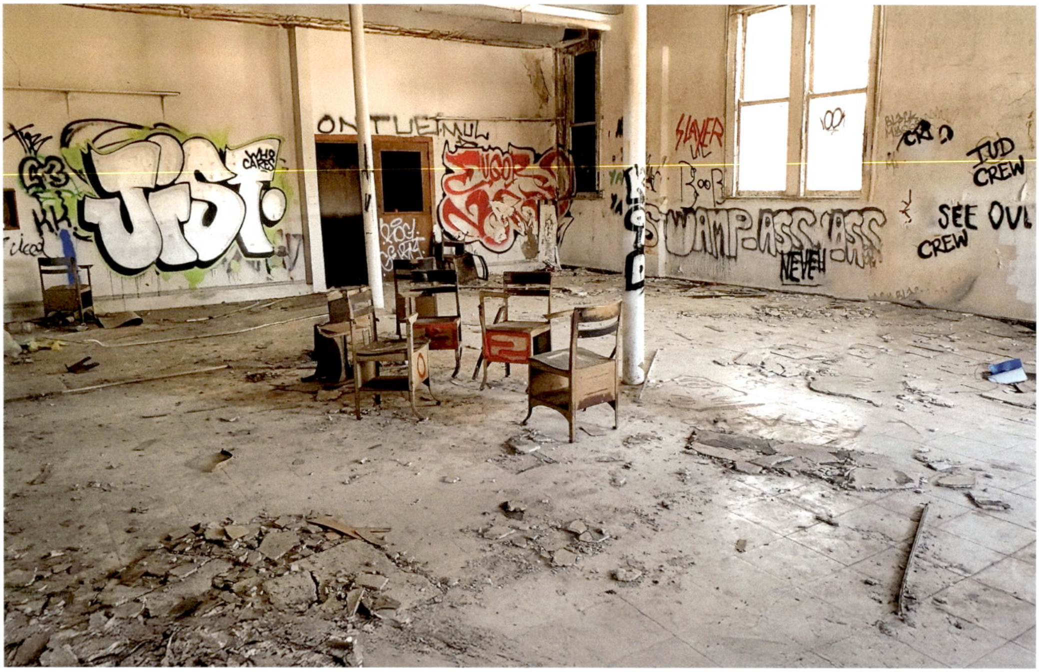

In one of the classrooms, rows of broken chairs sit in disarray, surrounded by graffiti and dust-covered walls.

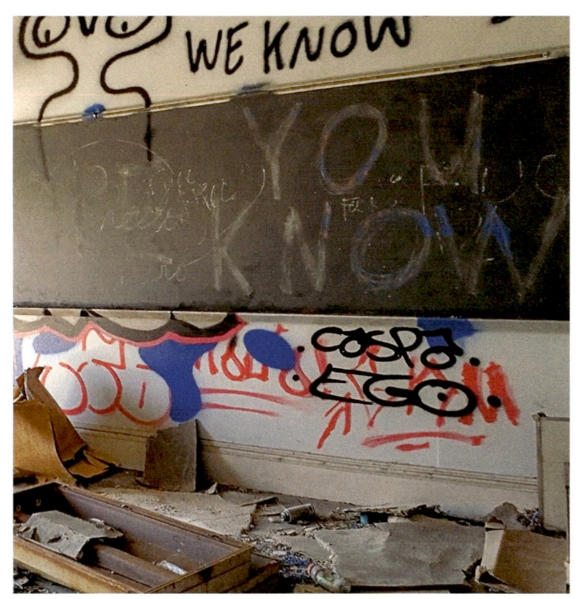
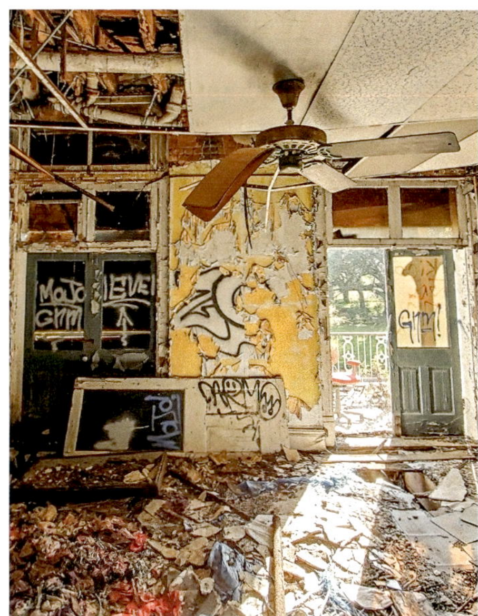

Above left: A chalkboard in another classroom remains covered in graffiti instead of lessons. The once vibrant space of learning has fallen into disrepair, where the echoes of students' voices have been replaced by silence and spray-painted messages

Above right: Sunlight peeks through an open doorway, illuminating the peeling paint, exposed wires, and debris-covered floor.

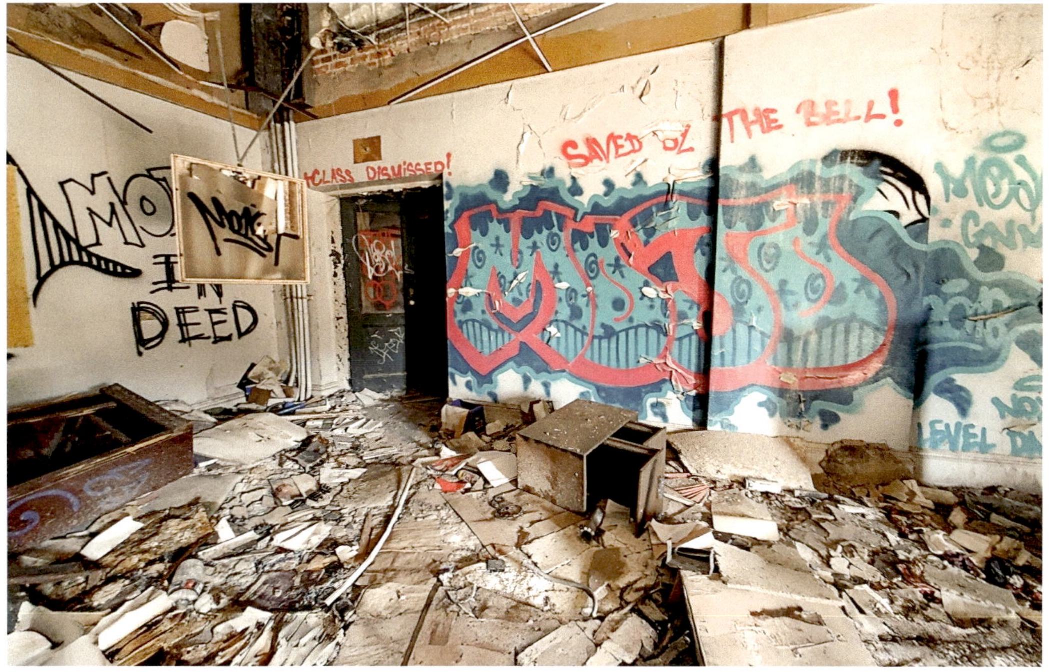

One of the classrooms is strewn with debris, old books, and graffiti-covered walls. A broken light fixture frame hangs, while the words "saved by the bell!" hint at a time when this room was filled with eager students.

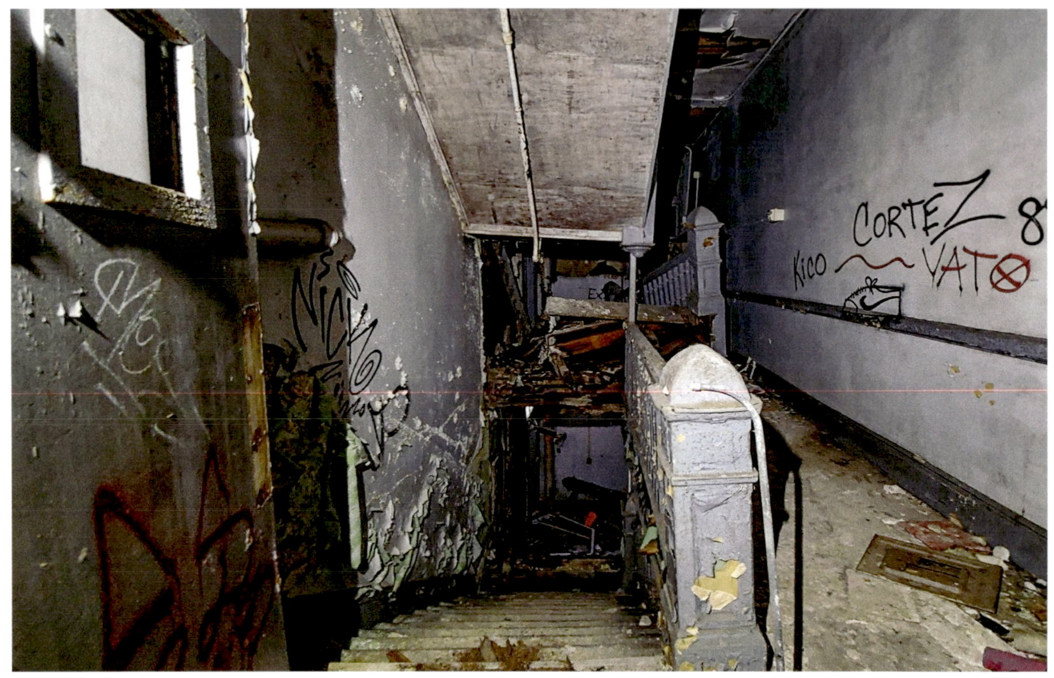

This once-beautiful staircase now leads only to darkness and rubble. With collapsing ceilings, it is a haunting reminder of the structure's former glory, now overshadowed by years of neglect.

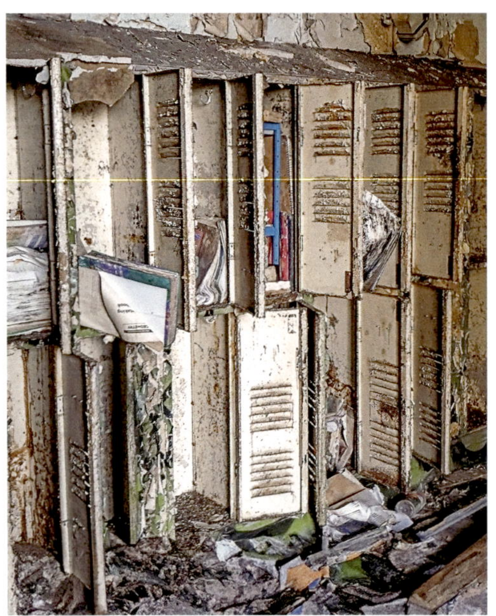

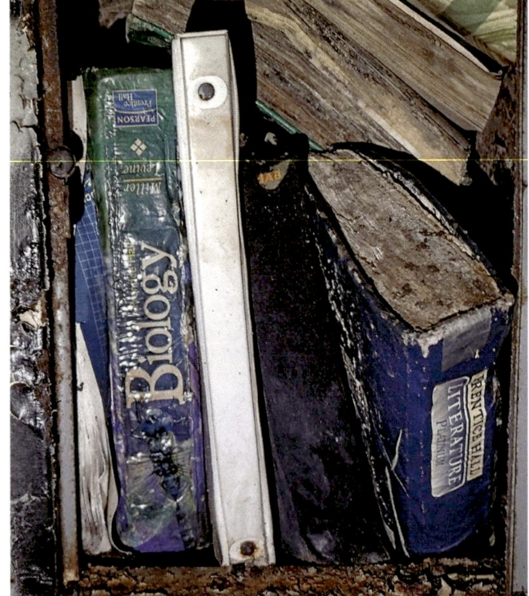

Above left: The rusted lockers still hold tattered books and forgotten belongings.

Above right: Hidden in one of the old, rusted lockers, old textbooks like *Biology* and *Literature* remain untouched for decades, their pages moldy and spines worn.

8

HOPE HAVEN ORPHANAGE

The Rise, Fall, and Controversy of a Marrero Sanctuary

Located in Marrero, Louisiana, across the Mississippi River from New Orleans, Hope Haven Orphanage still stands, once as a pillar of support and care for children in need. The Preservation Resource Center of New Orleans reports that in 1924, the Dibert Administration Building was built as part of the Hope Haven campus. This building included classrooms, dorms, and a chapel. In 1929, two wings were added which included more dorms and a dining area.

Also part of the large property is the Chinchuba Institute for the Deaf, established in the late nineteenth century. It was a pioneering institution in Louisiana for the education and care of deaf children. Founded by Father Hyacinthe Mignot, who initially used his Saint Clair Plantation home near the village of Chinchuba in what is now Mandeville, Louisiana. Another addition, Madonna Manor, was built across the street in 1932. This was to accommodate the growing number of students including girls along with the students from the Chinchuba Institute.

Despite its outward appearance of benevolence, Hope Haven Orphanage faced serious allegations of abuse and misconduct. Former residents began to come forward with claims of physical and emotional abuse perpetrated by staff members. These allegations included reports of harsh disciplinary measures, neglect, and mistreatment.

According to several NOLA.com articles, the accusations led to a series of investigations and legal actions. In the early 2000s, multiple lawsuits were filed against the Archdiocese of New Orleans, alleging that the institution had failed to protect the children from abuse and had covered up the misconduct. The legal battles revealed disturbing details about the conditions at the orphanage and the experiences of those who had lived there.

In 2003, several former staff members were indicted and arrested on charges related to the abuse allegations. The cases brought to light the severe shortcomings in the oversight and management of the orphanage, leading to public outrage and demands for accountability. The scandal had a profound impact on the reputation of Hope Haven, overshadowing the institution's earlier accomplishments.

The fallout from the abuse scandal, combined with declining financial support and changing social attitudes towards institutional care, contributed to the eventual closure of the residential portion of the orphanage. By the late 1990s, the institution had already begun to face challenges in maintaining its facilities and operations. The legal issues exacerbated these difficulties, leading to a reduction in the number of residents and staff.

In 2005, Hurricane Katrina caused further damage to the already declining facility, so the decision was made to close Hope Haven permanently. The buildings fell into disrepair, with broken windows, crumbling walls, and overgrown vegetation overtaking the grounds.

Today, the deserted orphanage stands as a haunting reminder of its troubled past. The dilapidated structures and overgrown landscapes tell a story of neglect and decay, contrasting sharply with the institution's former role as a place of refuge. For former residents, the memories of Hope Haven are tinged with both gratitude for the support they received and pain from the abuse they endured.

This exploration proved challenging for the krewe. Many of the buildings, like the Julian Saenger Gymnasium and Madonna Manor, were sealed up tight, so we focused our efforts on two accessible structures: the Dibert Administration Building and the Chinchuba Institute for the Deaf.

Walking through these buildings, I could not ignore the weight of the pain left behind. Knowing the horrors that unfolded within these walls evoked a mix of sadness and anger. Usually, I enjoy uncovering the history of the places I explore, but this experience felt different. Definitely more somber and unsettling than others.

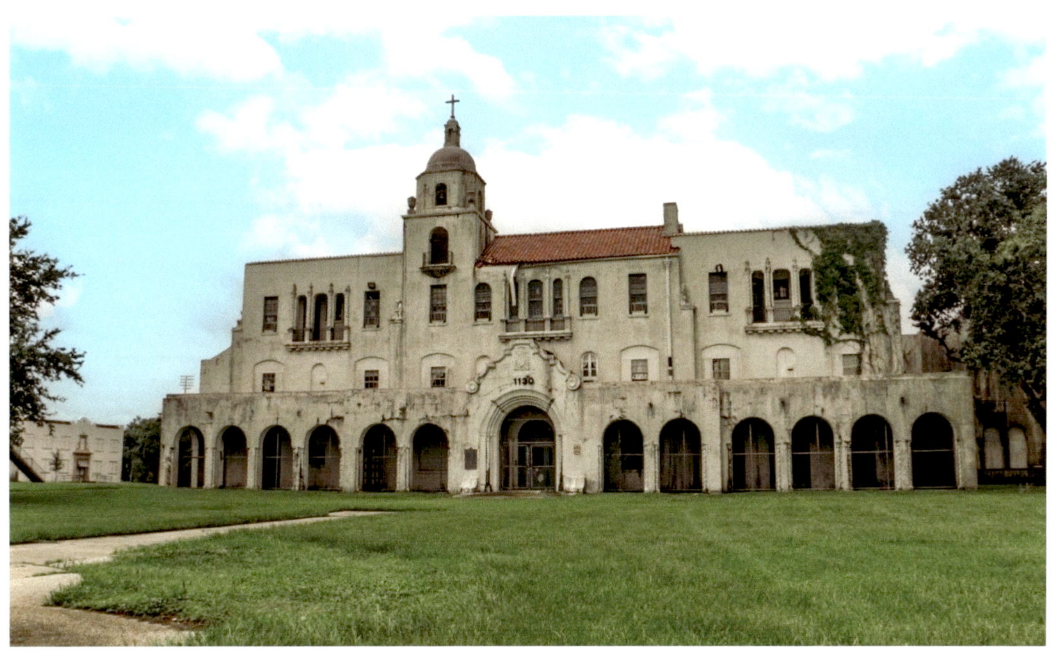

Hope Haven Orphanage, built in the 1920s in Marrero, served as a sanctuary for orphaned and troubled boys. The Dibert Administration Building now stands as a reminder of the hope it offered children, but also the terrible things that happened inside.

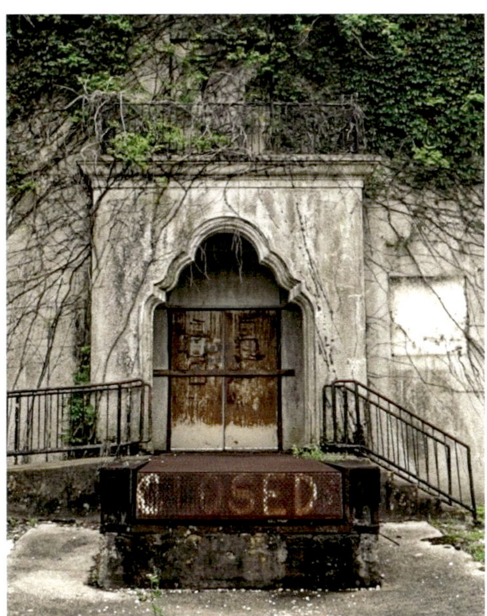

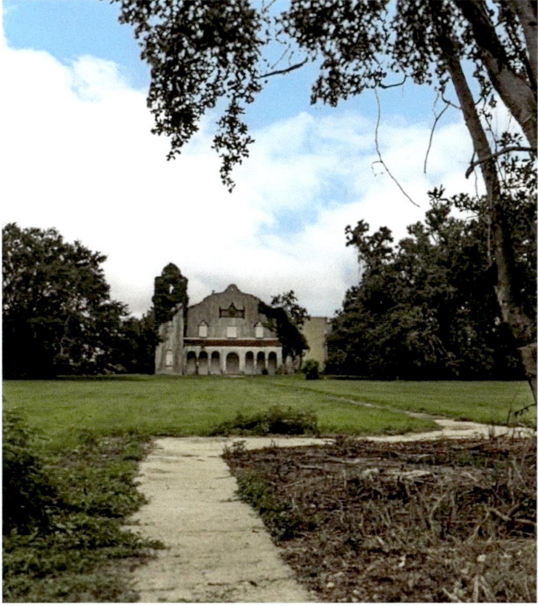

Above left: A sealed entrance, overgrown with creeping ivy, bears a rusted sign that reads "CLOSED." Once a place of refuge, these doors now remain firmly shut, standing as a symbol of the site's forgotten history.

Above right: The Julian Saenger Gymnasium, situated behind the Dibert Administration Building, once echoed with the sounds of youthful activity. Now, overgrown pathways are reminders of the vibrant community that once thrived here.

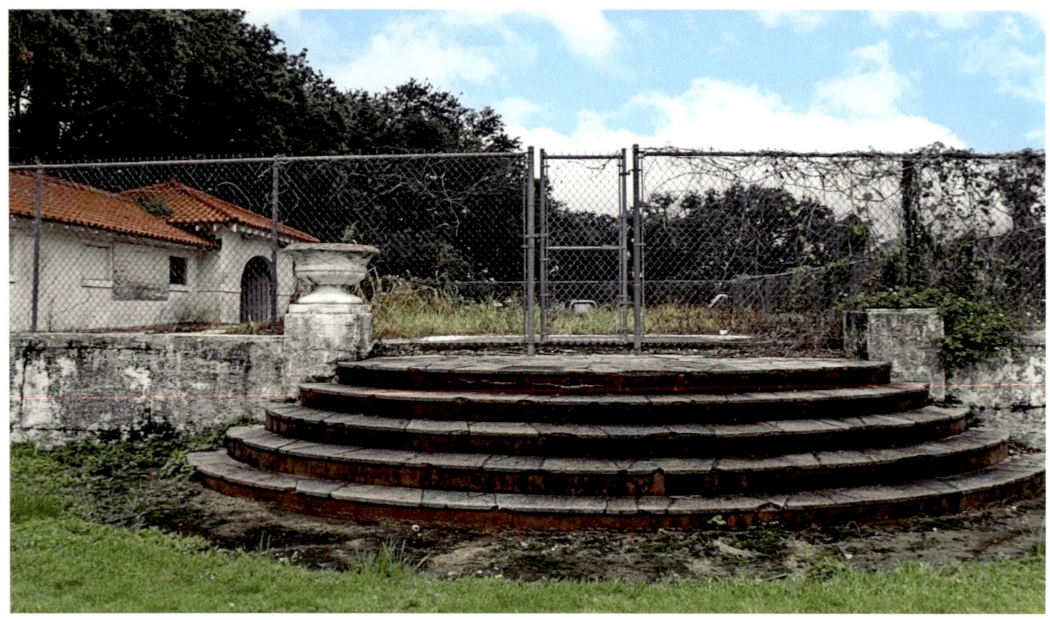

This filled-in swimming pool was once a part of the larger recreational facilities at Hope Haven. This area provided a place of respite for the children who called this place home.

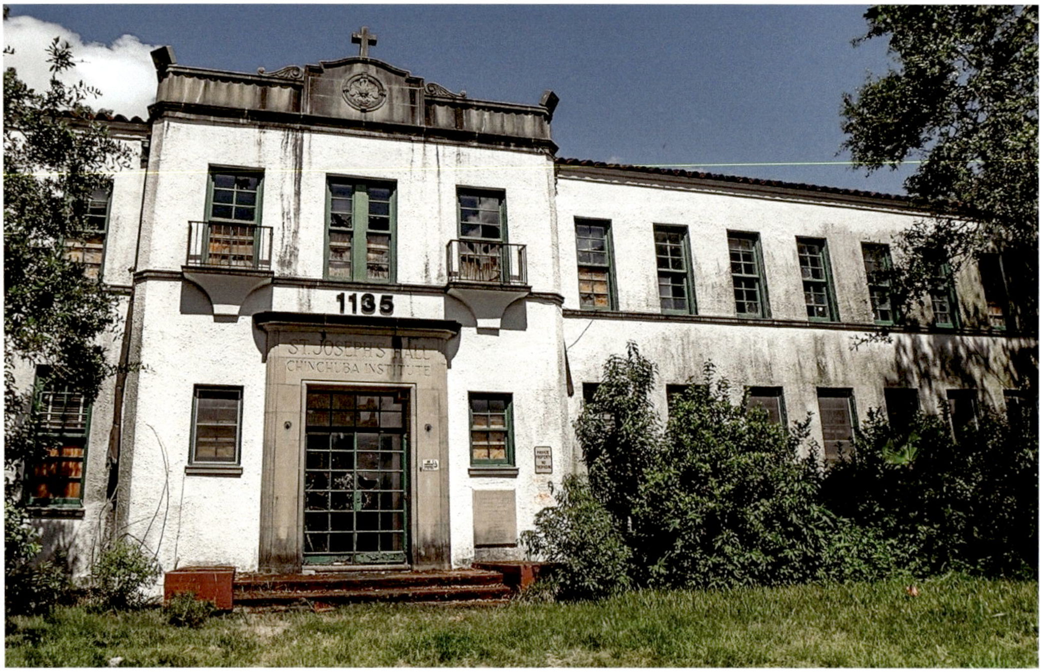

Chinchuba Institute for the Deaf, once a vital center for education and care, stands in disrepair across the street from the administration building. Its mission to serve the hearing-impaired community is now a distant memory, with its grounds overgrown and its structure weathered by time.

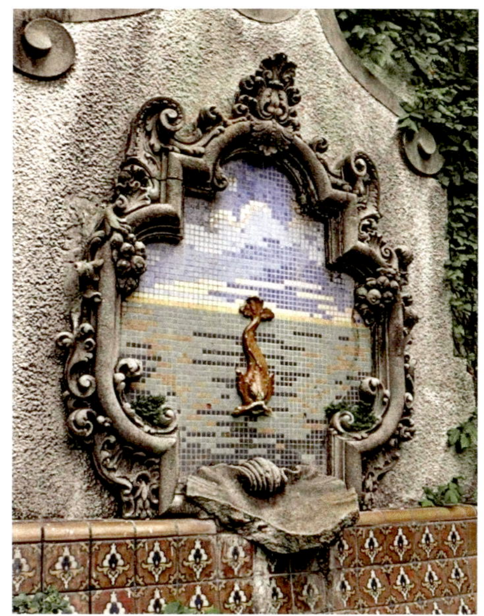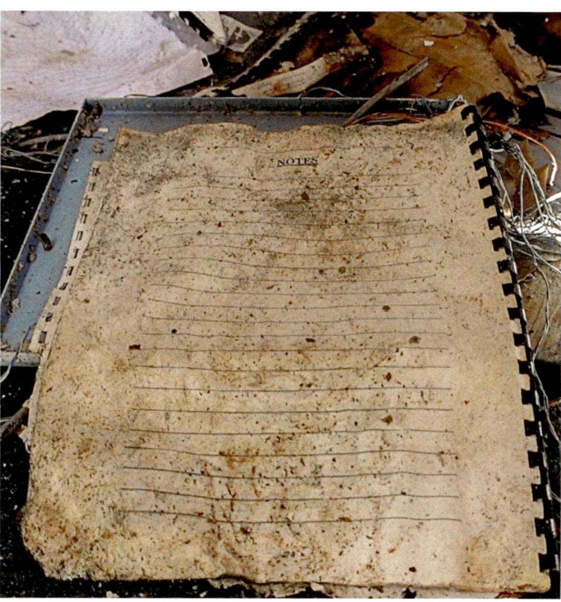

Above left: An ornate mosaic fountain in one of the courtyards of the administration building adorned with intricate tile work and decorative flourishes, now stands weathered and overgrown.

Above right: An empty, moldy notebook lies forgotten among the rubble. It had a purpose for notes and ideas, but the blank, dust-covered pages now serve as a reminder of unfinished stories left behind when the place was deserted.

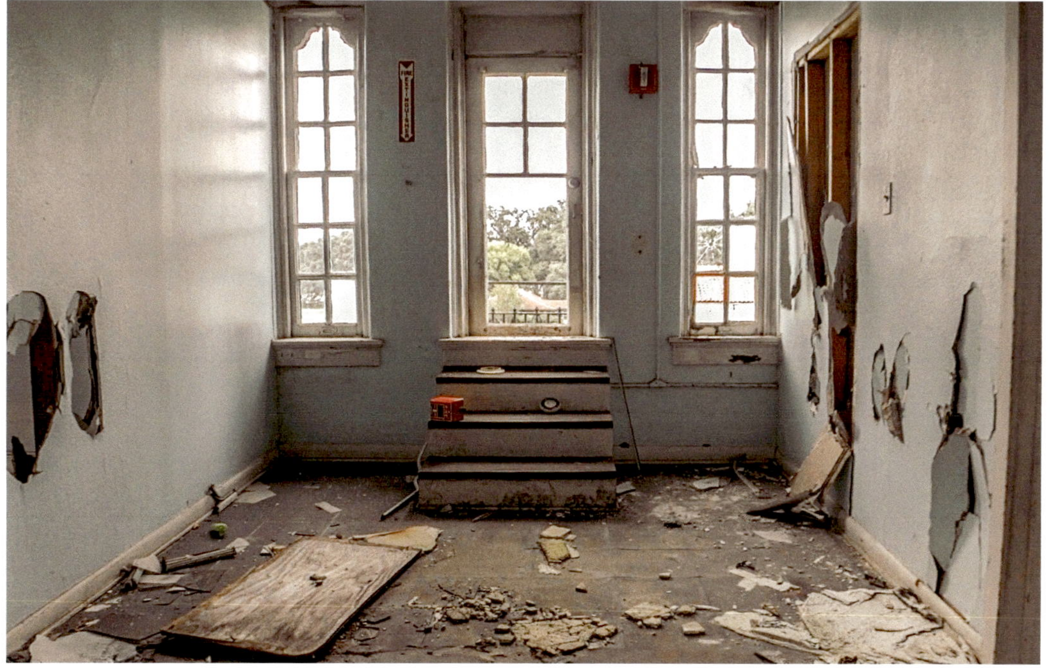

This once-bright corridor now stands empty and deteriorating. Sunlight streams through the arched windows, illuminating crumbling walls and debris scattered on the floor.

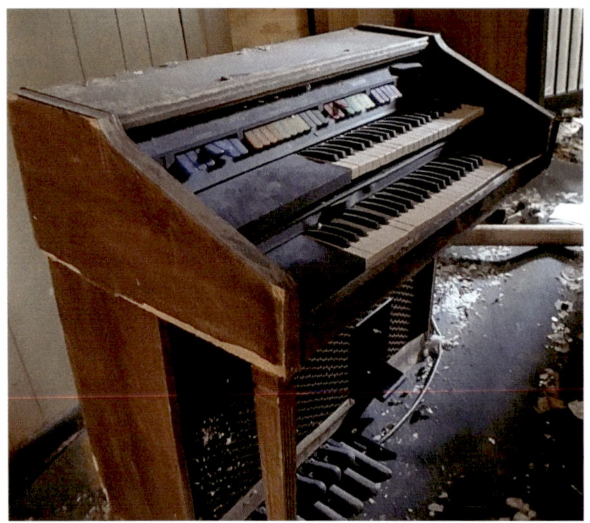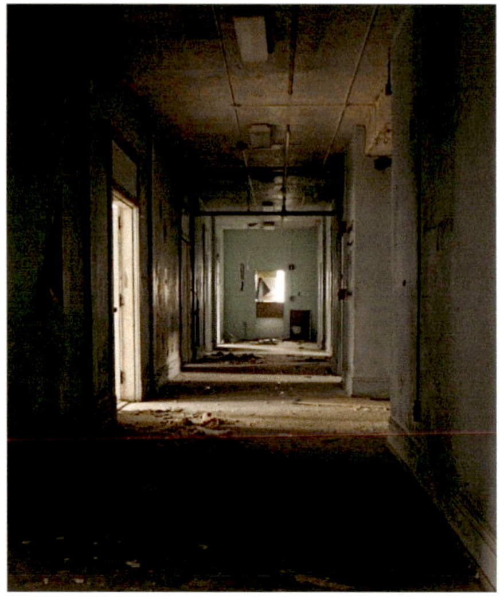

Above left: Inside a small chapel in the Chinchuba Institute building, an old organ sits forgotten amid the debris, its once-joyful melodies silenced by years of neglect.

Above right: The long, dimly lit hallway stretches into silence. Once filled with the footsteps of staff and children, it now lies bathed in a soft, muted light that only accentuates the emptiness left behind.

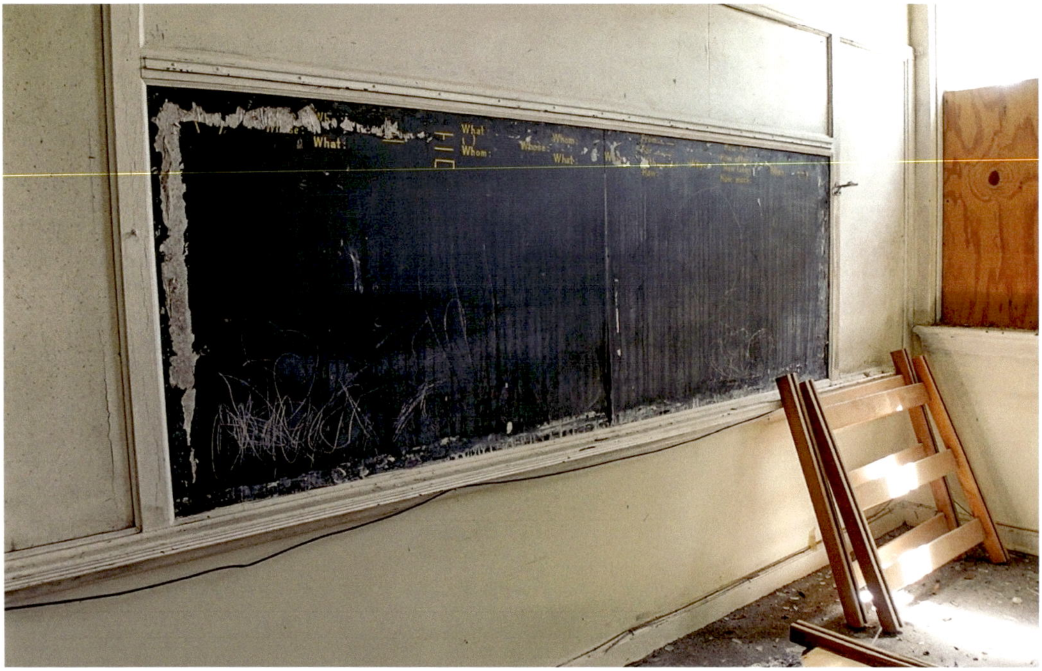

An old chalkboard in one of the classrooms remains, faded and covered with the last scribbles from its past occupants and few people that have ventured inside since.

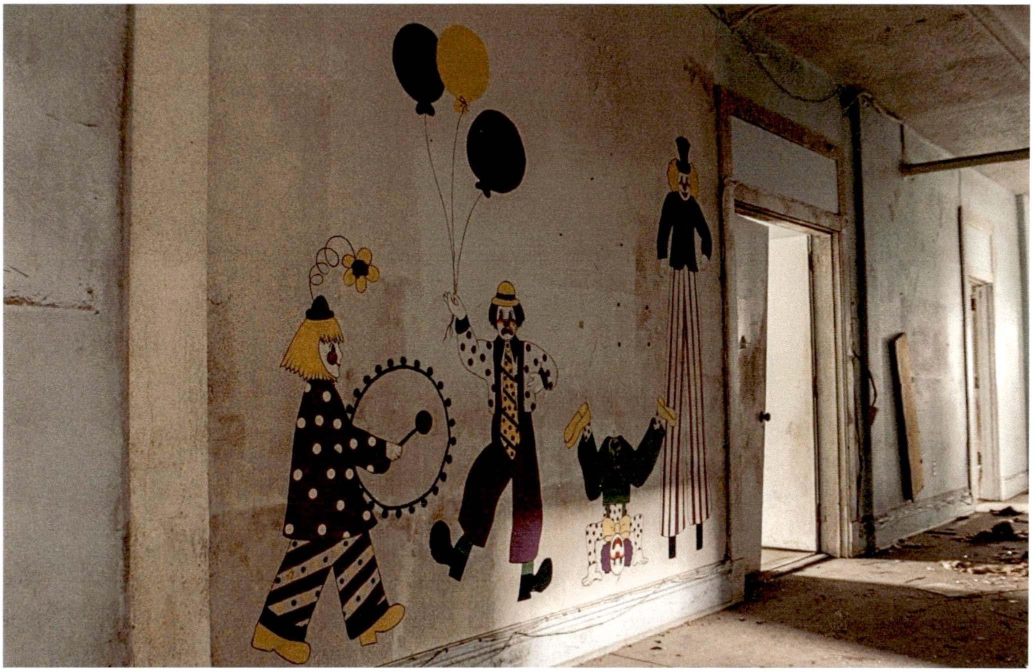

A whimsical mural of clowns and balloons still brightens the walls of the corridors. Intended to bring joy and comfort to children, the faded figures now stand eerily frozen in time.

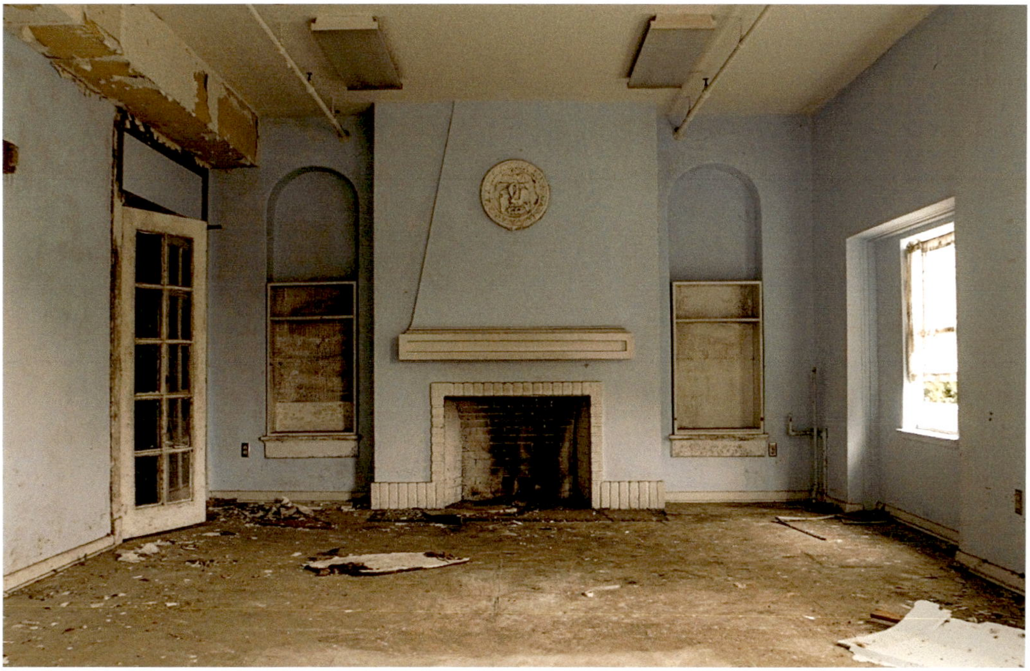

The once-cozy common room, centered around a now soot-stained fireplace, is a shadow of its former self. The walls, painted a calming blue, still bear the insignia of the institution.

9

LAFON HOME FOR BOYS

From Hope and Faith to Desertion

The Lafon Home for Boys was established with a mission to support and educate disadvantaged youth. The institution's story reflects themes of care, crisis, and eventual closure, highlighting both its impact and the challenges it faced over the years.

In 1893, philanthropist Thomy Lafon donated a building to the Sisters of the Holy Family, according to information gathered from AbandonedSoutheast.com. The building, designated for an all-boys' orphanage, was in response to an all-girls' orphanage that was opened the previous year. However, in 1933, a fire would destroy the orphanage buildings, and a new site was sought out.

The new building was dedicated in 1935 and was a Colonial-style building made of concrete and brick so it would be more resistant to fire. The new building, located in the Gentilly neighborhood, had enough room for up to 100 young boys to stay. The new orphanage offered a safe and supportive environment for orphaned boys.

The orphanage would close in 1967 and reopen as the Lafon Child Development Center just two years later. Throughout its operation, it played a crucial role in the New Orleans community. It offered a structured environment where boys could receive education, vocational training, and engage in recreational activities. The focus on holistic development aimed to equip the children with the skills and knowledge needed for independent living.

The devastation wrought by Hurricane Katrina marked a turning point for the facility. The storm's impact caused extensive damage to the structure and disrupted its operations. In the wake of the hurricane, the institution struggled to recover and maintain its services amid the broader chaos of the disaster's aftermath.

Ultimately, the Sisters of the Holy Family were unable to overcome the challenges posed by the hurricane. The institution closed its doors permanently in 2005, marking the end of a significant chapter in New Orleans' child welfare history. It sat deserted ever since and was finally demolished in 2020 due to its deteriorating state.

This was one of my earliest explorations, and it certainly did not disappoint. The signs of vandalism were everywhere. Graffiti covered the walls, and many items were broken, including a statue of the Virgin Mary with its head missing. We searched for the head but never found it, adding to the creepy atmosphere of the site.

Unexpectedly, we encountered a police officer outside. After explaining to him what we were doing, he simply advised us to be careful and mentioned he would check back on us later, a rare and surprising interaction in the world of urban exploration.

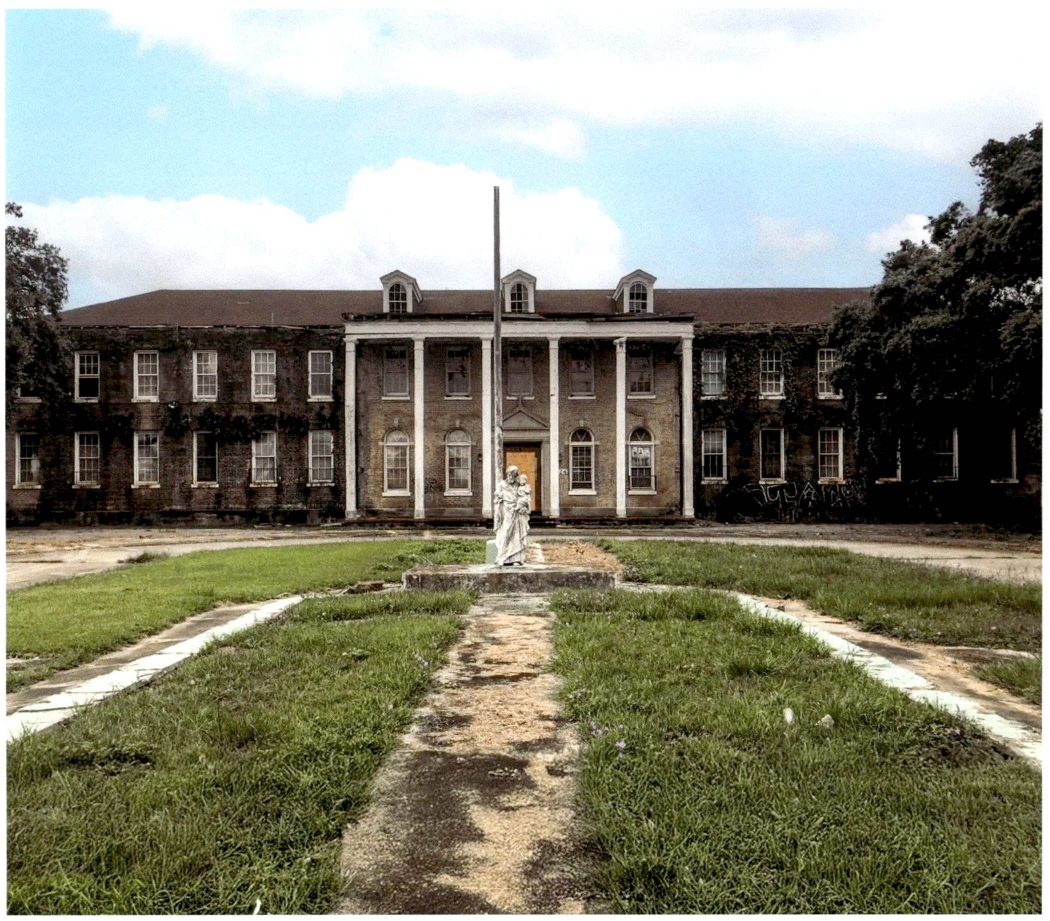

Established in the early 1900s, the Lafon Home for Boys once served as a refuge for orphaned and underprivileged children in New Orleans. The grand brick building, complete with stately columns and a serene statue out front, was intended to offer hope and stability. Closed in 2005 due to Hurricane Katrina, it sat deserted until it was demolished in 2020.

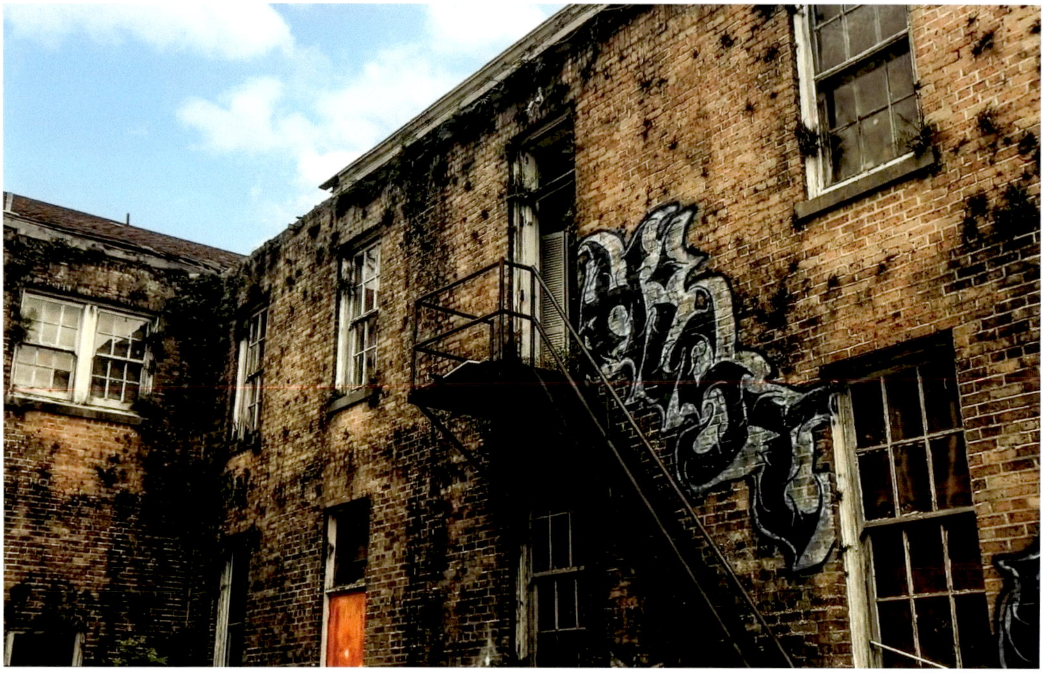

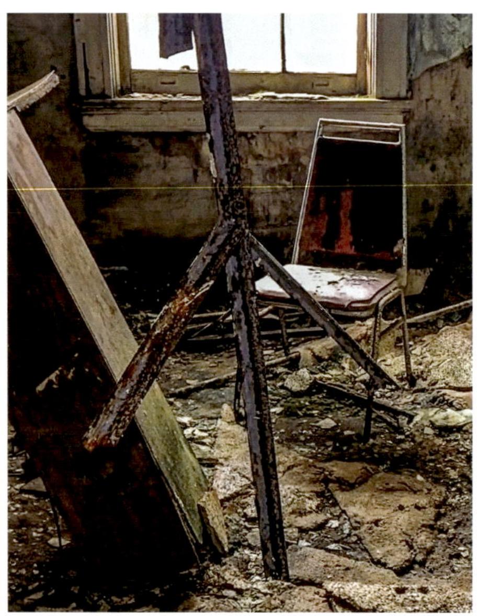

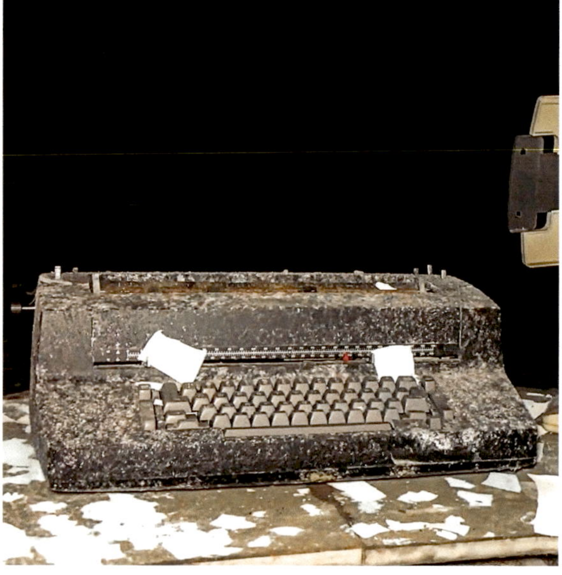

The rear of the old building reveals the wear of years gone by, with ivy reclaiming its brick walls and graffiti adding layers to its story.

Above left: Inside, the remnants of a room lie scattered and decayed. Broken furniture, crumbling plaster, and rusted frames tell the story of a space that once housed children. The sunlight filtering through the grime-covered windows casts a dim glow on what has been left behind.

Above right: An old typewriter sits on a dusty desk. A relic from the past that hints at the administrative work that once took place here, perhaps documenting the lives of the children who called this place home. Now, it lies coated in dust.

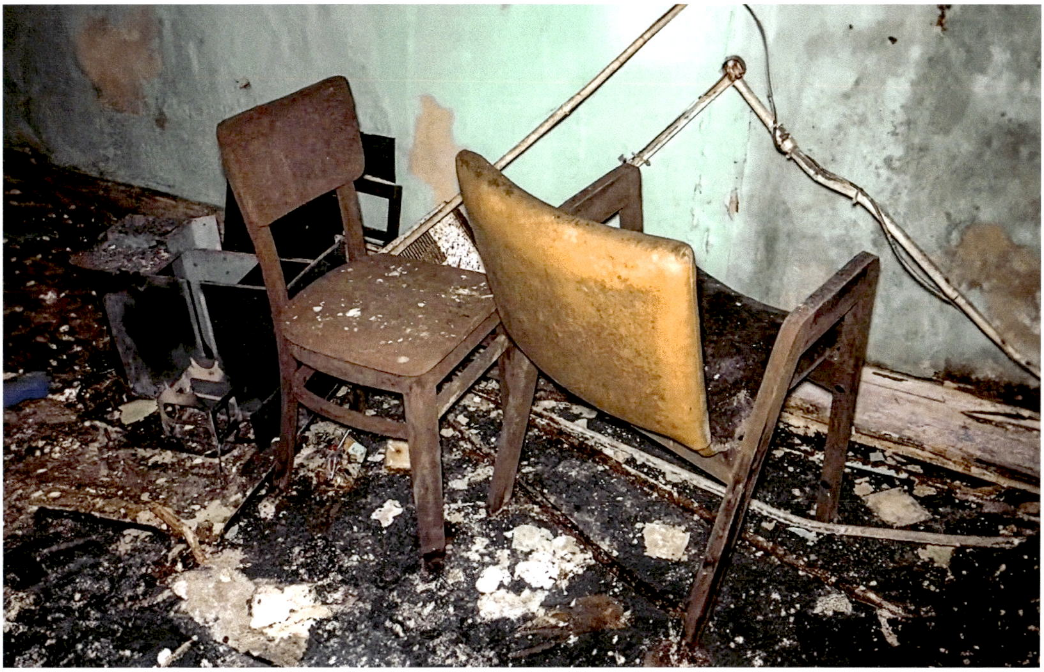

Two worn chairs, long forgotten, rest against a peeling wall. These humble seats may have once hosted conversations among staff or served as a place for a child to rest.

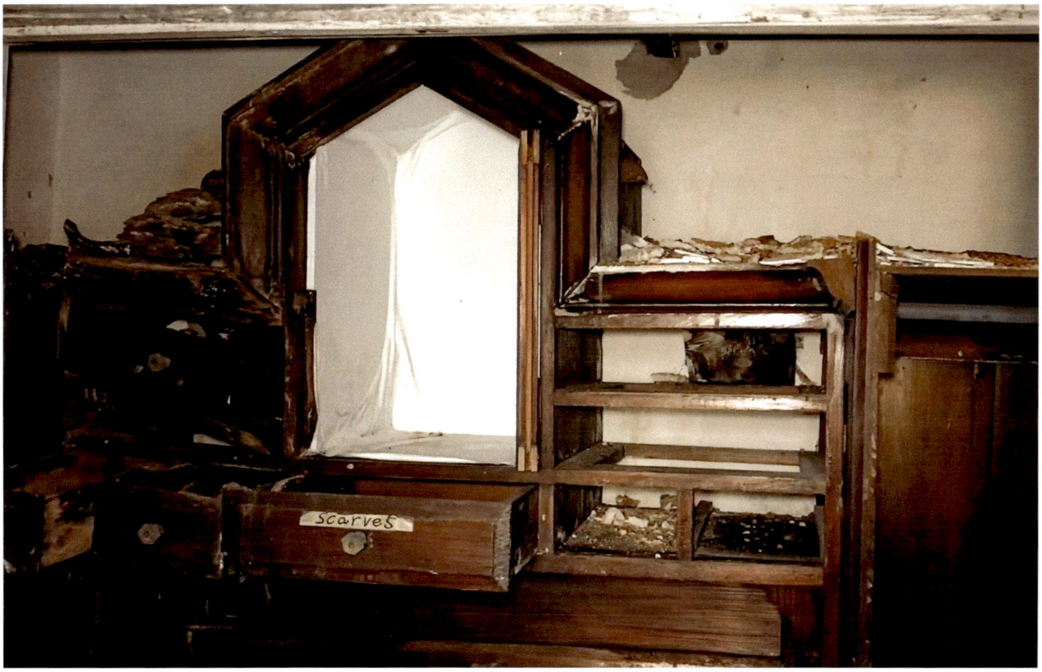

An old cabinet sits in a closet, its drawers now ajar and labeled with remnants of its former organization. The word "scarves" is still faintly visible on one drawer, hinting at the careful order that once governed this space.

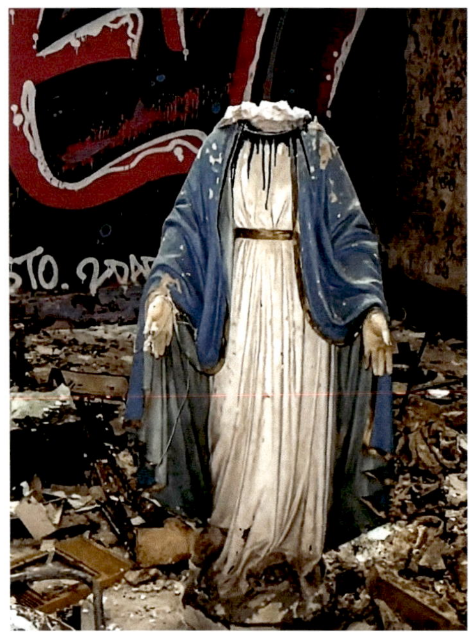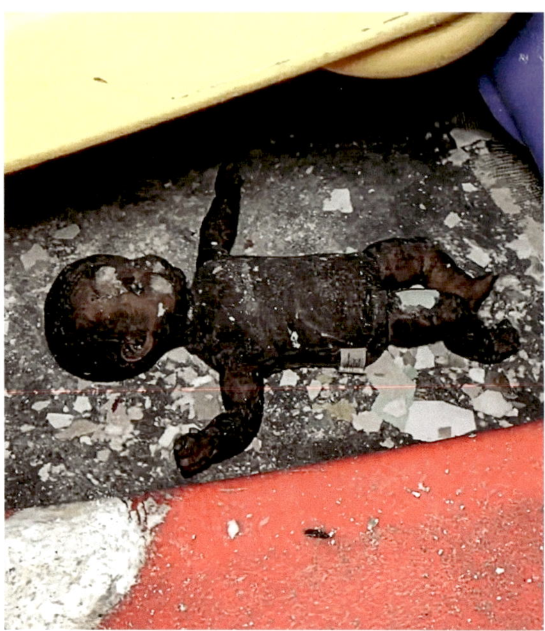

Above left: The krewe came across this headless statue of the Virgin Mary. Once a symbol of comfort and protection, it now stands among graffiti-covered walls and a floor strewn with shattered remnants.

Above right: A lonely doll lies on the floor among the dust and debris.

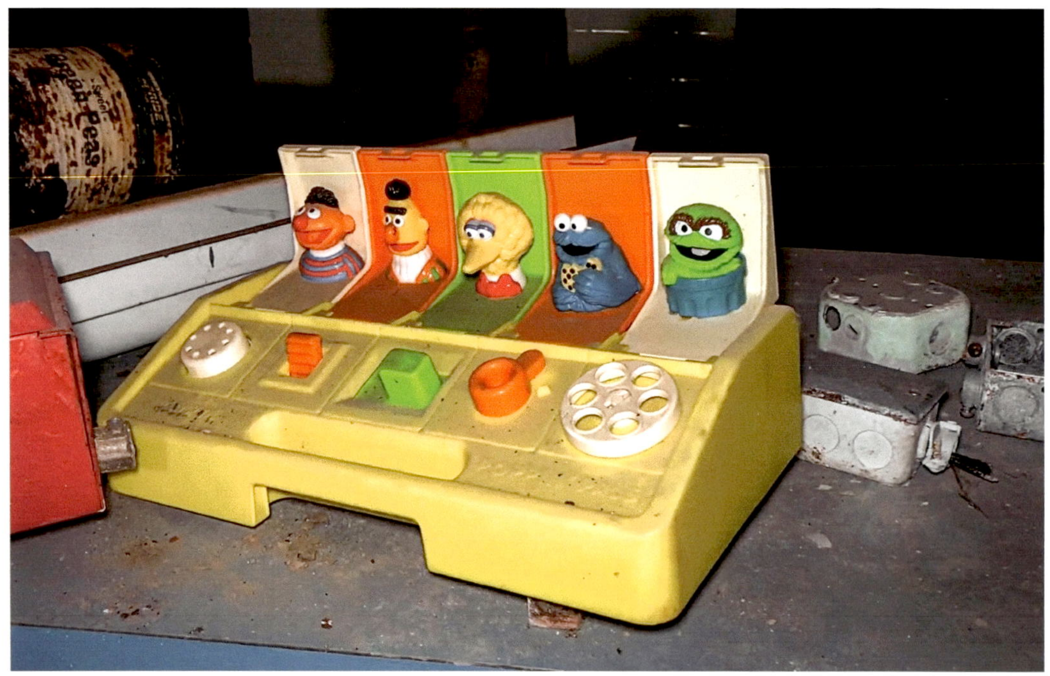

A forgotten toy featuring beloved Sesame Street characters sits on a dirty table. The cheerful faces of Bert, Ernie, and friends seem out of place amid the surrounding decay.

10

LINDY BOGGS MEDICAL CENTER

A Beacon of Care, Lost to Katrina's Wrath

Per Nolaghosts.com, Lindy Boggs Medical Center was originally established as Mercy Hospital in 1926, named in honor of the Sisters of Mercy. The hospital provided critical medical services to the community, embodying the values of compassion and care central to its mission.

In 1992, the hospital underwent a major transformation and was renamed Lindy Boggs Medical Center in honor of Lindy Boggs, a prominent Louisiana native and former U.S. Representative. The renaming was part of a broader effort to revitalize the hospital and continue its legacy of service under a new banner. Despite the name change, the facility maintained its commitment to providing comprehensive healthcare to the community.

When Hurricane Katrina struck in 2005, it faced catastrophic challenges. The storm's devastation severely impacted the hospital, leading to extensive damage to the facility. The powerful winds and flooding overwhelmed the hospital's infrastructure, causing significant operational disruptions.

In the immediate aftermath of the hurricane, the hospital struggled to provide care amid the chaos. The facility's operations were severely hindered by the loss of power, damage to medical equipment, and the destruction of critical infrastructure. The generators were located in the basement, and because of the flooding from the storm, they were damaged and could not provide the backup power for the building. They were forced to evacuate patients and staff, losing many lives in the process.

In the months following, the hospital faced immense challenges as it attempted to recover. The facility encountered severe difficulties in securing the necessary resources and repairs to resume full operations. Despite efforts to restore services, the extensive damage and financial strain proved overwhelming.

One of the most persistent issues was the basement of the medical center, which remained flooded long after the storm. The basement, crucial for housing various hospital systems and equipment, was inundated with water, creating ongoing challenges for the facility. The basement remained flooded for sixteen years until some of the water was finally pumped out in an effort to begin remediation of the building.

The krewe returned to this hospital multiple times to ensure we explored every inch possible. Because the water had recently been pumped out, we were able to access the basement, which had been submerged for over sixteen years at the time. Despite being drained, the space was still wet, filthy, and coated in mud, with debris of all kinds scattered about.

Most things made of metal had either rusted beyond recognition or disintegrated entirely. The most fascinating and surreal discovery in the basement was the old morgue, complete with intact doors and drawers that once held bodies. Standing in that space, imagining its former use, was an unforgettable and surreal experience.

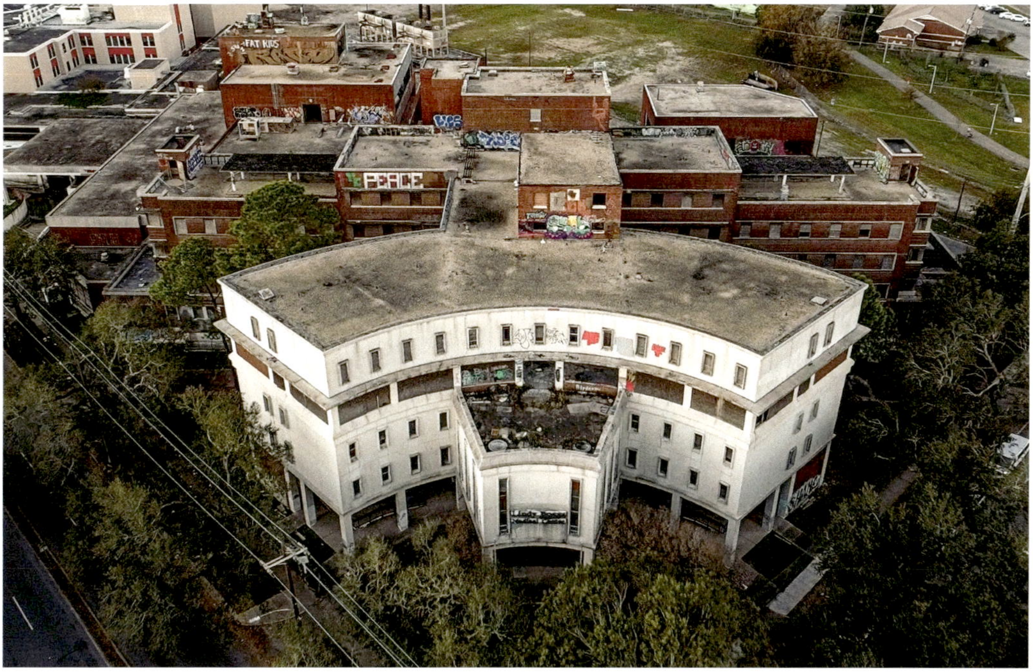

The Lindy Boggs Medical Center originally opened in the 1920s as Mercy Hospital. This sprawling complex once provided critical care to the community.

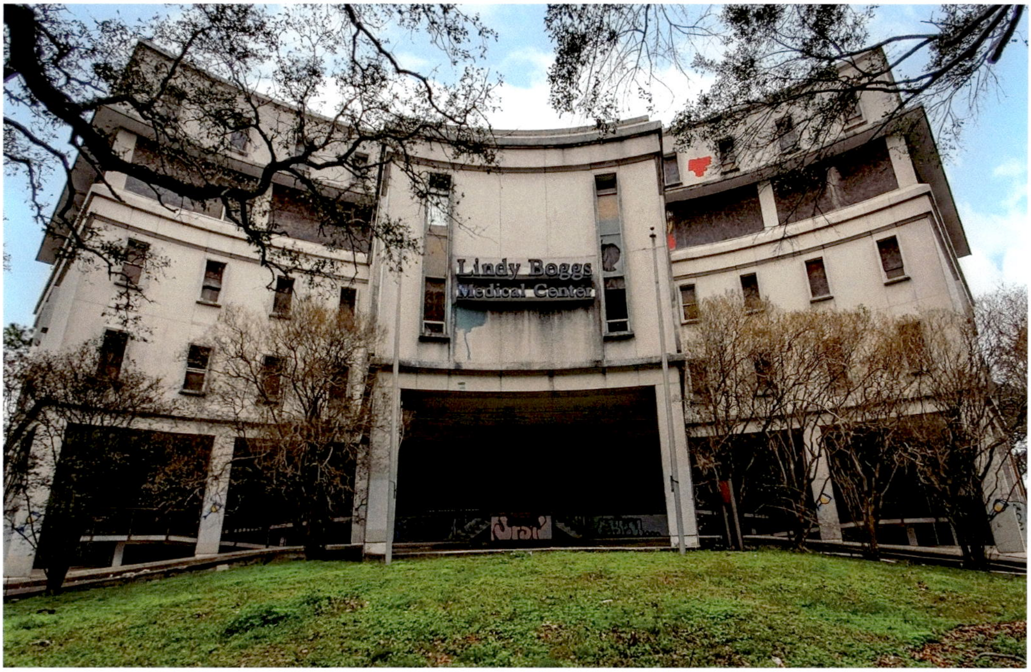

The front entrance now stands eerily silent. The hospital, named after the beloved Louisiana congresswoman, served the community for decades until it was forced to close in 2005.

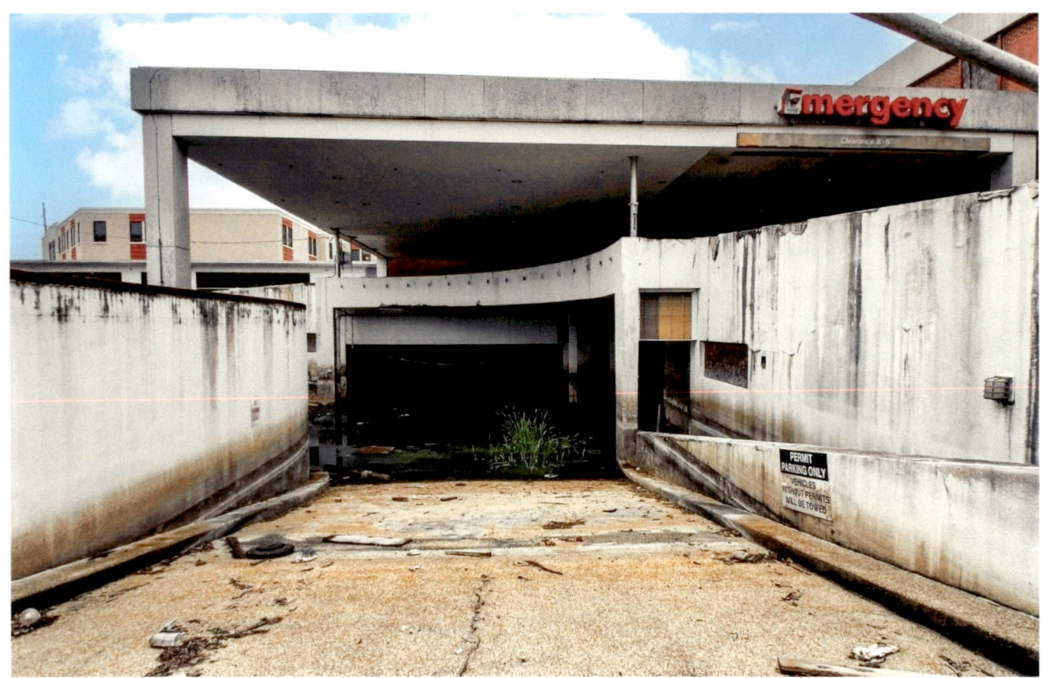

The emergency entrance is now overgrown and the bottom area flooded. A place where ambulances rushed in to save lives now sits quiet and deserted.

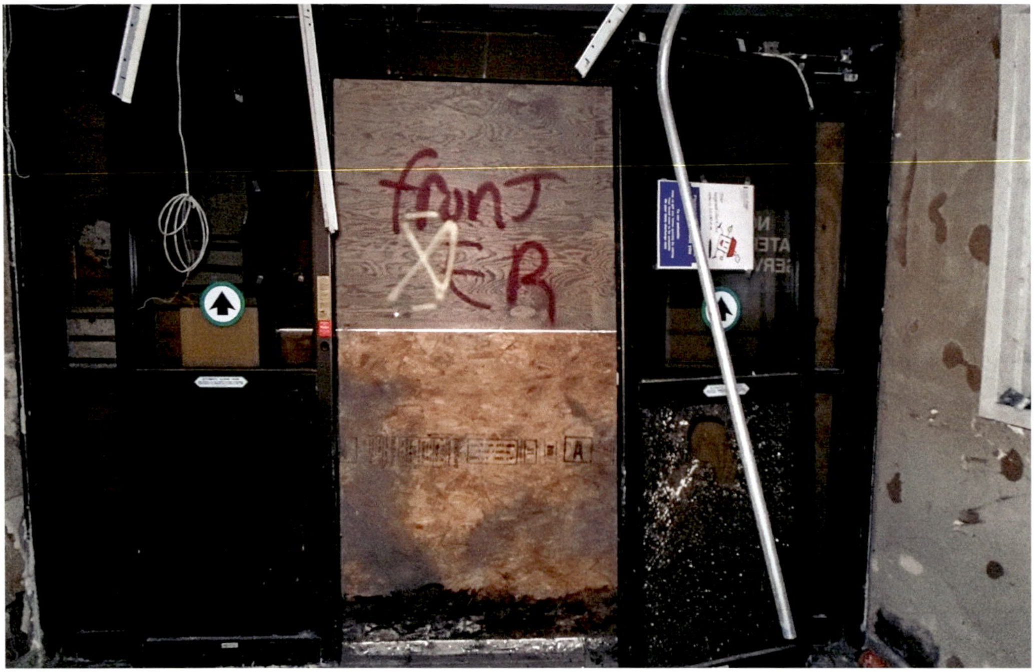

On the inside, the entrance to the emergency room is boarded up and vandalized. Faded signs and broken glass hint at the hospital's previous role as a place of healing.

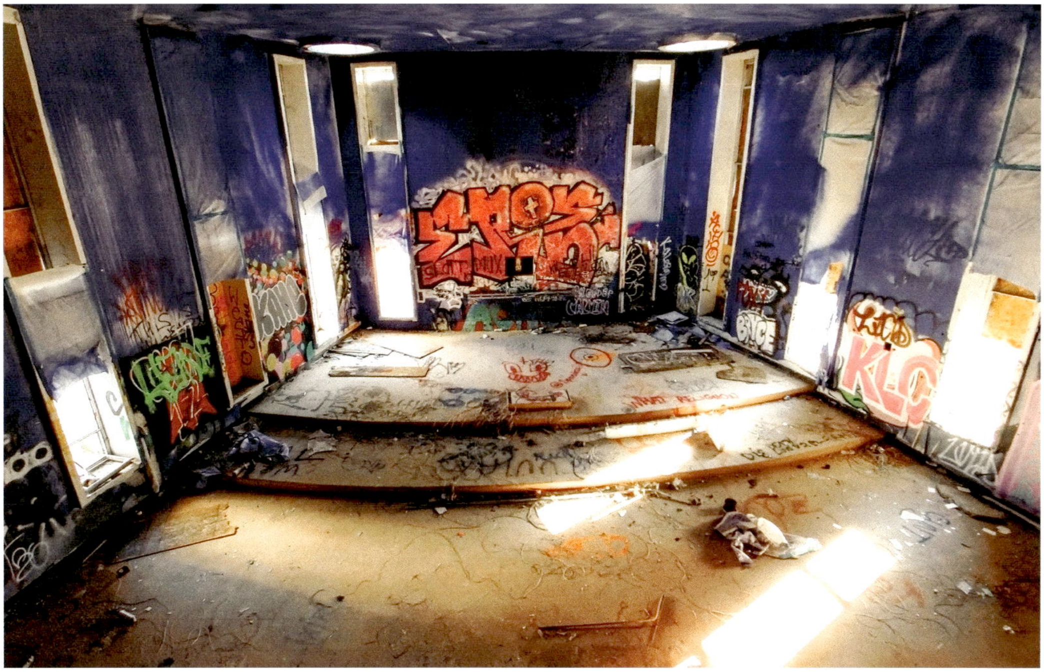

This once-serene chapel has been transformed into a canvas for graffiti artists. The vivid blue walls and stained floors stand in contrast to the room's original purpose as a place of solace and reflection.

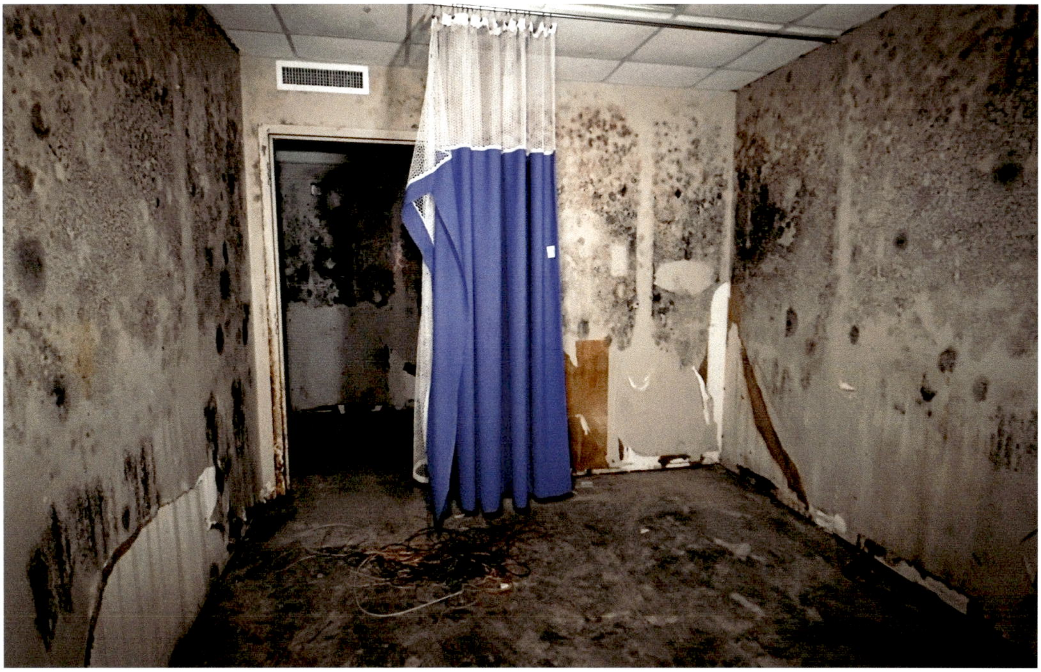

In one of the hospital rooms, we find it is now overrun with black mold. A faded blue privacy curtain still hangs, a haunting reminder of the patients who once occupied this space.

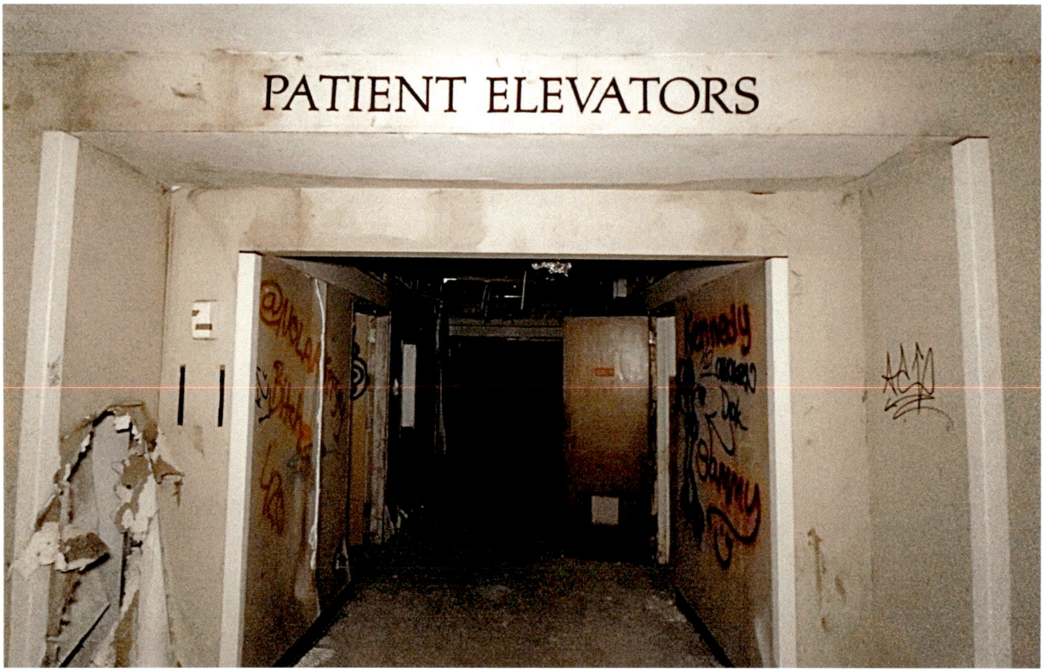

PATIENT ELEVATORS

The dimly lit hallway leading to the patient elevators is now cloaked in darkness and graffiti.

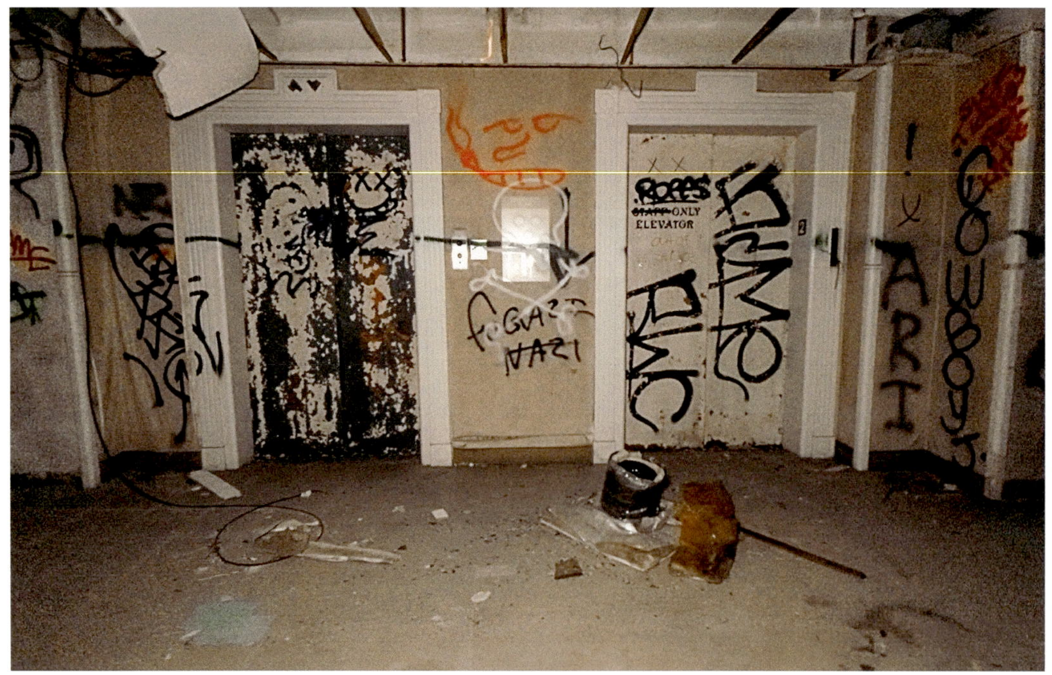

The elevators once transported patients, doctors, and staff throughout the hospital. The peeling paint and vandalized doors are reminders of the years of neglect since the building was deserted decades ago.

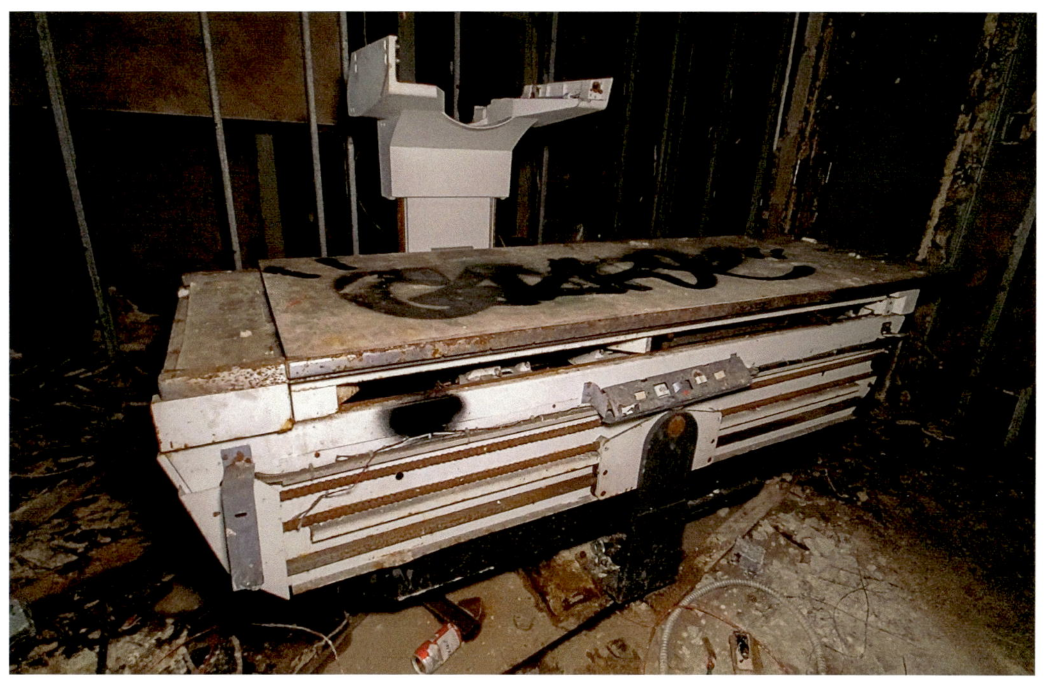

An imaging table used to position patients for X-rays and other diagnostic procedures, now sits unused in a decaying room. The control panels, once vital for precision in capturing images, are now rusted and broken.

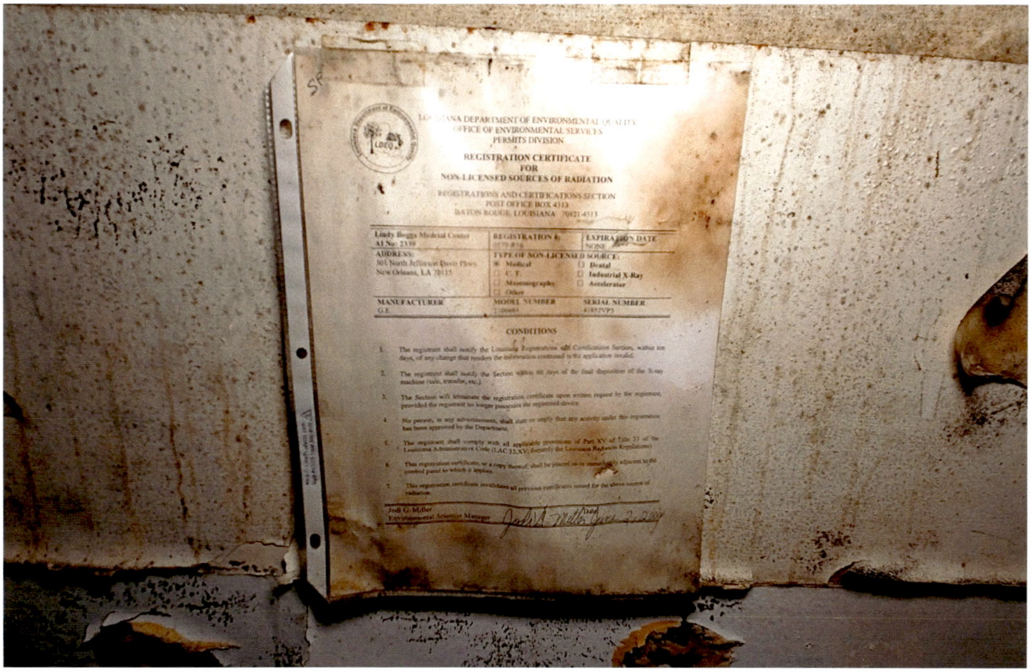

A faded radiation certificate still clings to the wall, documenting the hospital's compliance for non-licensed sources of radiation. Issued by the Louisiana Department of Environmental Quality, the certificate once ensured that X-ray machines and imaging equipment operated safely within the hospital.

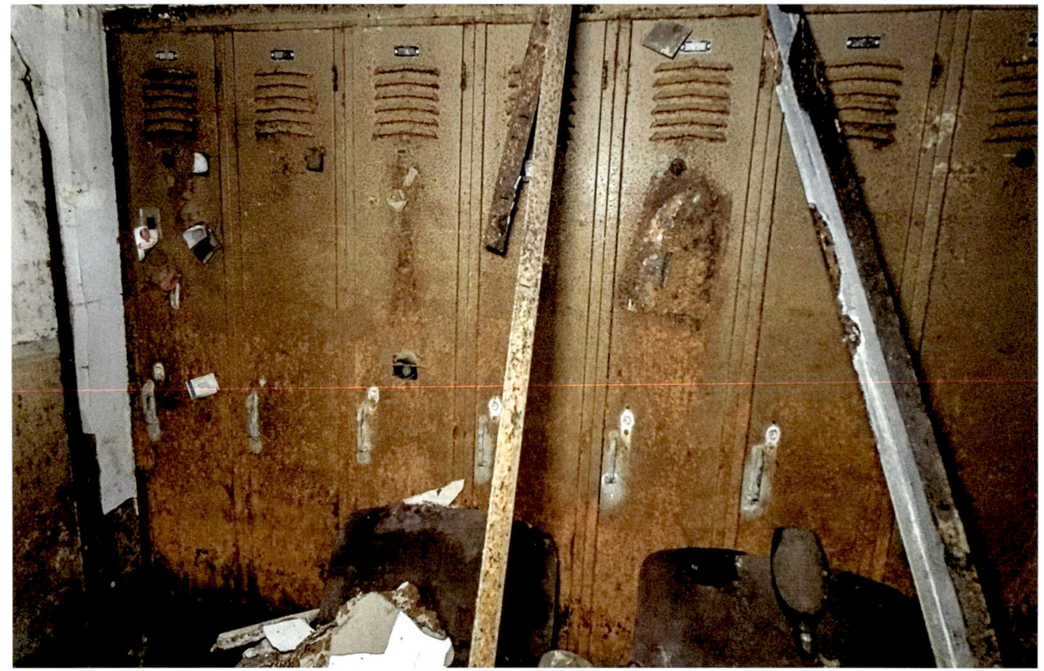

The krewe made our way to the basement that had been submerged underwater for almost twenty years. The water only recently had been pumped out. Through all the nasty wet muck and grime, we found these rusted lockers. The contents inside, once used by hospital staff, are now relics bearing the marks of years spent underwater.

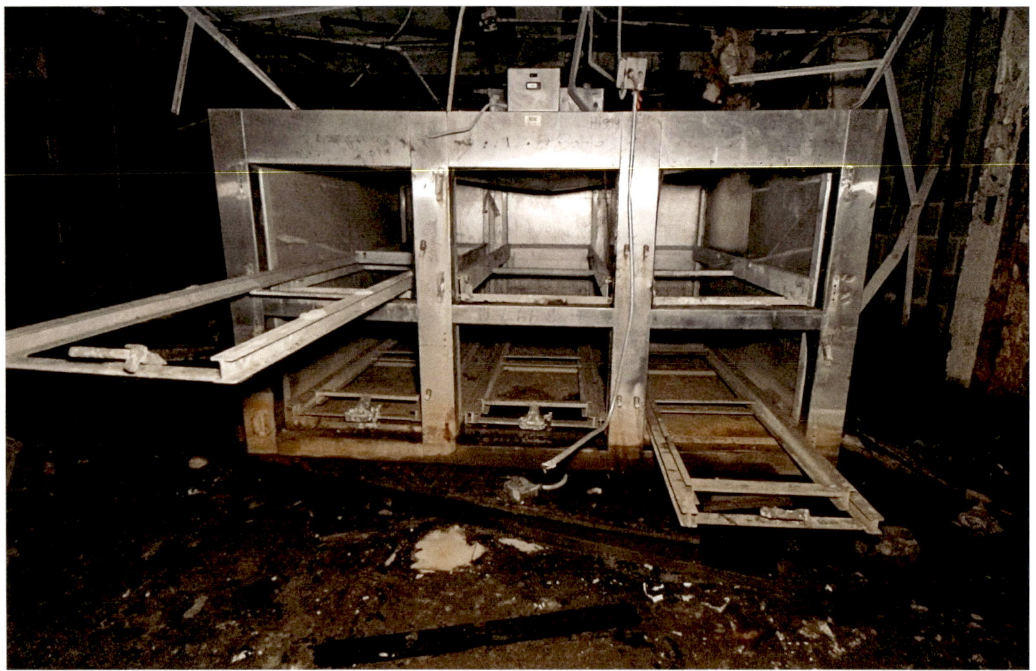

We also found the morgue which had been submerged as well. The once-sterile, stainless-steel drawers stand open, their interiors rusted and stained. The floodwaters have long receded, but the damage left behind serves as a chilling reminder of the hospital's abrupt closure, leaving these rooms to be forgotten in the depths below.

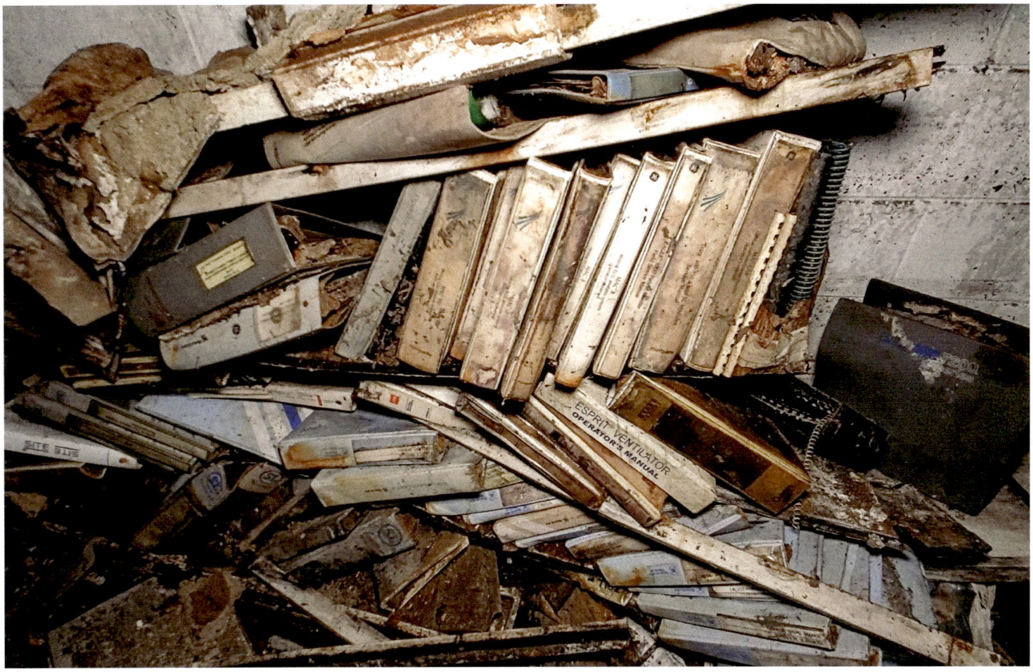

A pile of waterlogged manuals and documents were found left behind in one of the large closets in the once-flooded basement.

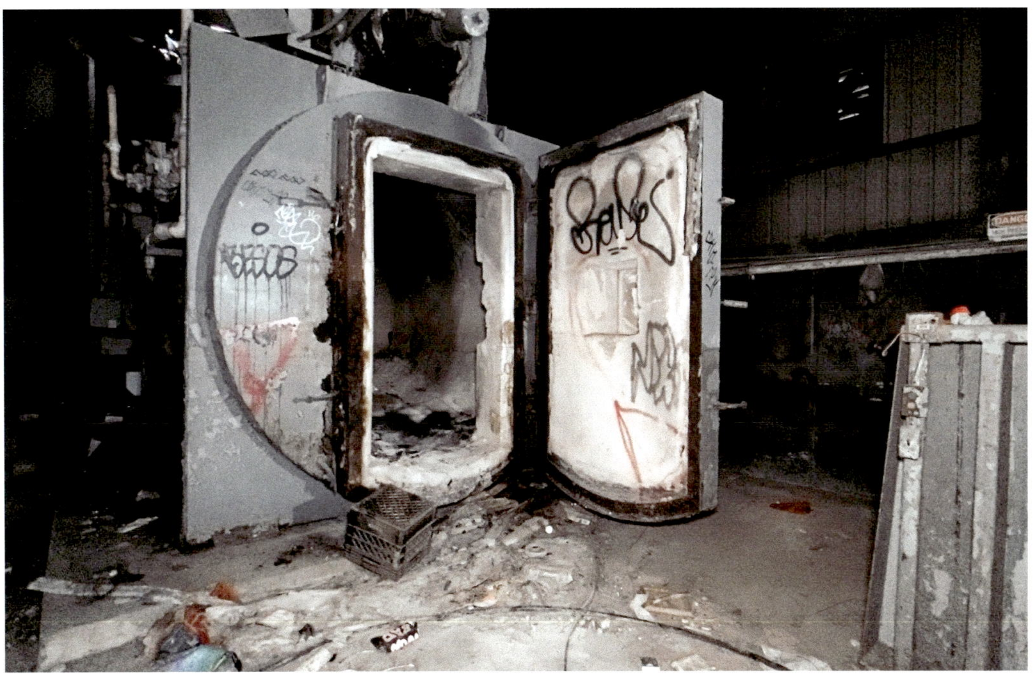

In a separate building, we found an industrial incinerator. Once used for the disposal of medical waste, the heavy doors now hang ajar, revealing an interior long forgotten. The smell of burned items still emanated from within the small space.

11

THE TIMES-PICAYUNE NEWSPAPER PLANT

Extra! Extra! Read All About It!

The Times-Picayune building, once an iconic structure in New Orleans, held a prominent place in the city's journalistic history. The building, located at 3801 Howard Avenue, was the headquarters of *The Times-Picayune*, New Orleans' primary newspaper. Its story spans from its establishment as a beacon of local news to its eventual demolition, reflecting both the evolution of media and the changing urban landscape.

Research from NOLA.com and old issues of the *Times-Picayune* shows that the newspaper was established in 1837 and became a staple of the city's media landscape, chronicling local, national, and international news for over a century. The newspaper's presence was a cornerstone of New Orleans' public life, shaping public discourse and providing a record of the city's history.

The building itself was a notable example of mid-twentieth-century architecture, featuring a modernist design that symbolized the newspaper's prominence and commitment to journalism. Constructed in the 1950s, it housed the editorial offices, printing presses, and other facilities necessary for a major newspaper operation. The structure became a landmark in its own right, embodying the growth and influence of the newspaper.

As the media industry underwent significant changes in the late twentieth and early twenty-first centuries, the newspaper faced challenges similar to those encountered by many traditional newspapers. The rise of digital media, shifting reader habits, and economic pressures led to a decline in print circulation and advertising revenue. The Times-Picayune, like many of its counterparts, grappled with these transformations.

In 2012, the newspaper made headlines itself when it announced a significant shift in its operations, transitioning from a daily print publication to a digital-first model with reduced print frequency. This change marked the beginning of a new era, focusing on digital content and online engagement rather than traditional print distribution.

With this transition and the subsequent relocation of its operations, the building became increasingly obsolete. The newspaper moved to a new smaller location leaving the iconic building deserted and for sale. It became yet another playground for urban explorers and photographers, as well as squatters and criminals.

The property was eventually purchased, and demolition of the building began in 2019, bringing down a structure that had once been a symbol of the city's journalistic heritage. The demolition was a poignant moment for many in New Orleans, reflecting the broader trends affecting traditional media and the changing urban landscape.

When we visited, demolition had already begun on one section of the building. Growing up in New Orleans and reading *The Times-Picayune* for as long as I can remember, it was surreal to step inside the place where those newspapers were once printed. Though the massive printing machines were long gone, the vast printing room remained, and being there was an unforgettable experience.

We even attempted to climb the clock tower, but the old, rusted spiral staircase became increasingly unstable as we ascended. Prioritizing safety, we decided not to push our luck and turned back before reaching the top.

After our visit, demolition continued, and we watched as the building was dismantled piece by piece. Like much of the city, we tuned in to witness the iconic clock tower brought down with a dramatic explosion, captured live for all to see. It was a bittersweet end to a piece of New Orleans' history.

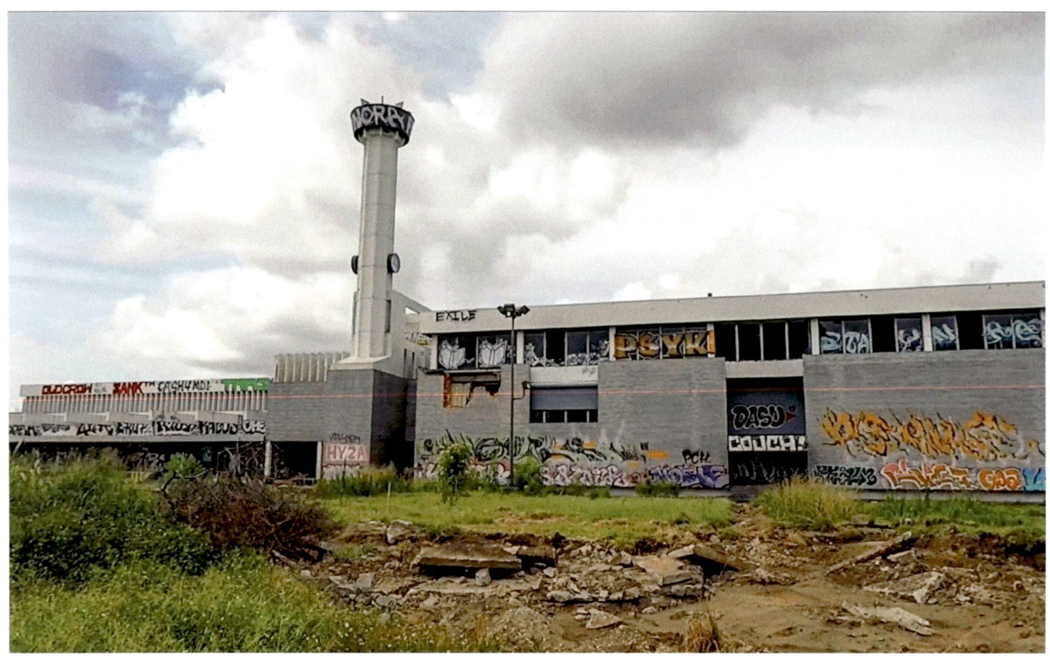

The Times-Picayune building, once the hub of New Orleans' renowned newspaper. The iconic clock tower, still towering above the deteriorating structure, serves as a reminder of the stories and headlines that once shaped the city. Left vacant after the newspaper relocated, the building now endures in silence, surrounded by overgrown vegetation and crumbling pavement.

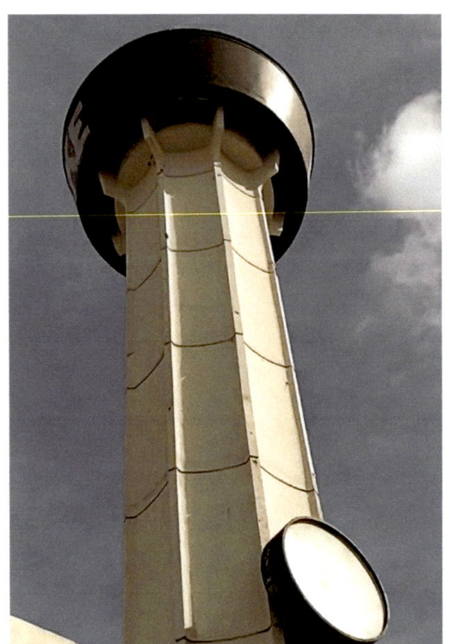

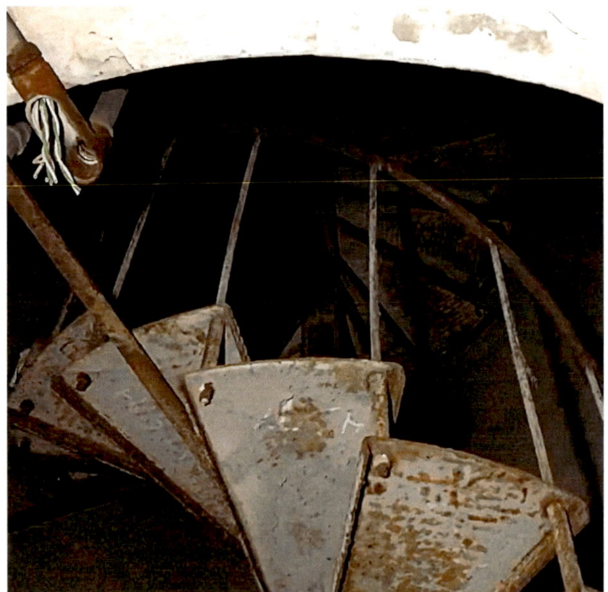

Above left: The iconic clock tower still reaches for the sky, its once-functional face now frozen in time. Graffiti surrounding the top of the tower indicated people had managed to climb to the top from the inside.

Above right: Inside the clock tower, a narrow spiral staircase winds upward into darkness. We made an attempt to climb to the top but out of safety chose to turn back about halfway up.

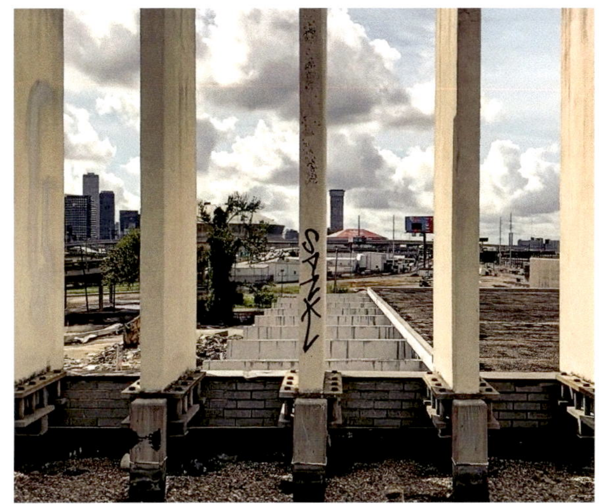
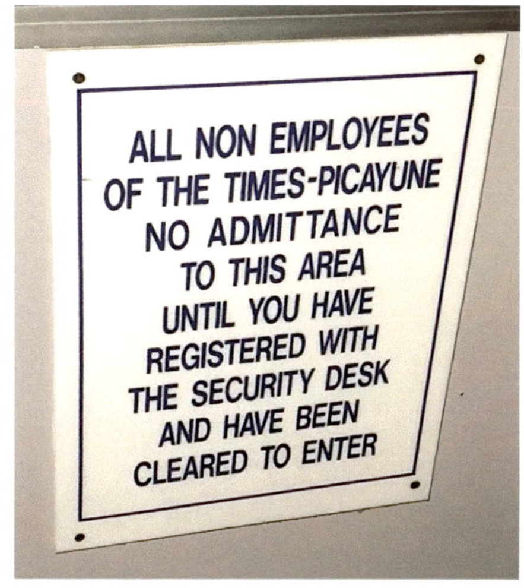

Above left: From the rooftop of the building, the New Orleans skyline stretches into the distance. The old newspaper headquarters now offers only views of a city that has moved on without it.

Above right: A faded sign still warns non-employees to check in at the security desk. The area now sits empty, with no security personnel to enforce its message.

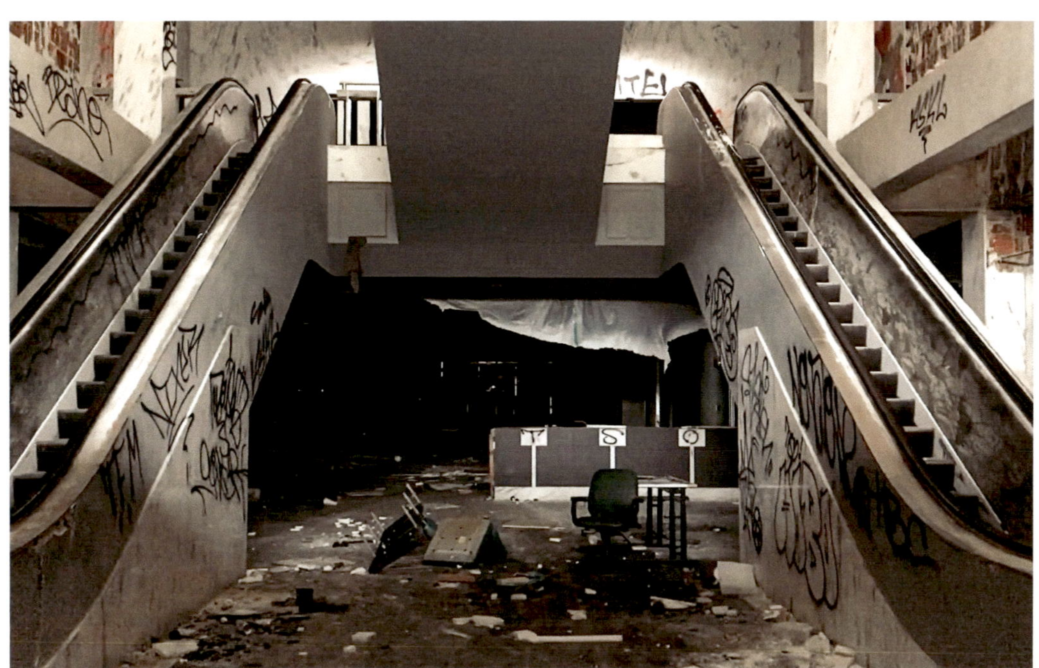

The main lobby where these escalators once greeted visitors with grandeur. The walls were at one time adorned with elegant marble sculpture murals, setting a prestigious tone for one of New Orleans' most influential news outlets. Today, the artwork is long gone, replaced with graffiti and signs of neglect.

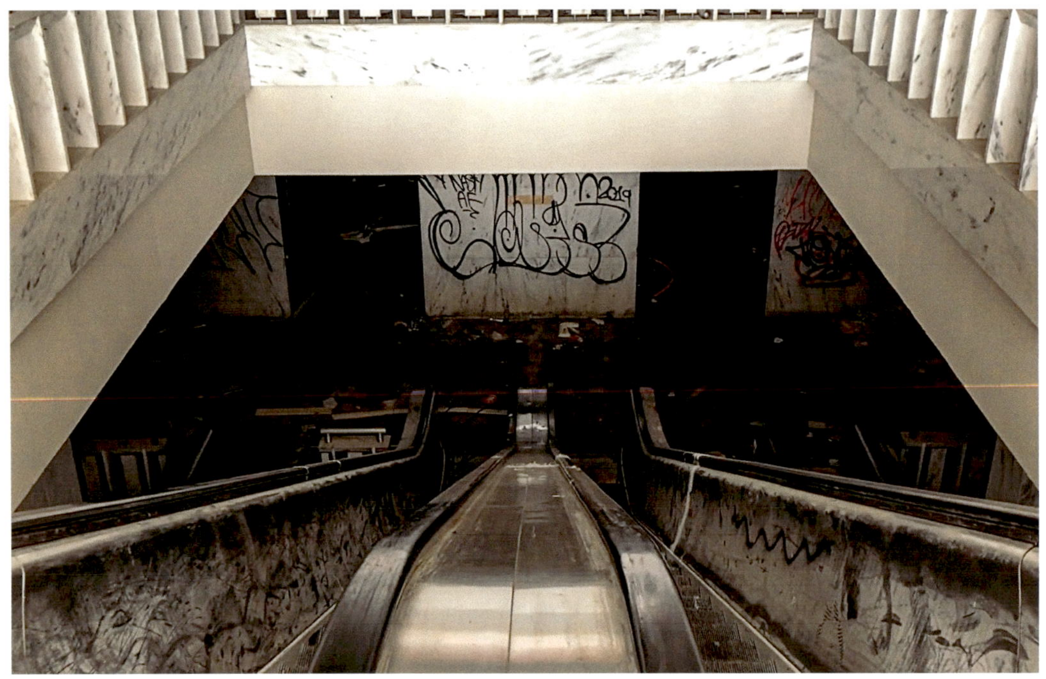

A view from the top of the grand escalators in the main lobby. The walls and railings, once clad in marble, now stand naked. This vantage point overlooks the remnants of what was once a prestigious gathering space for staff and visitors but now only sees darkness and decay.

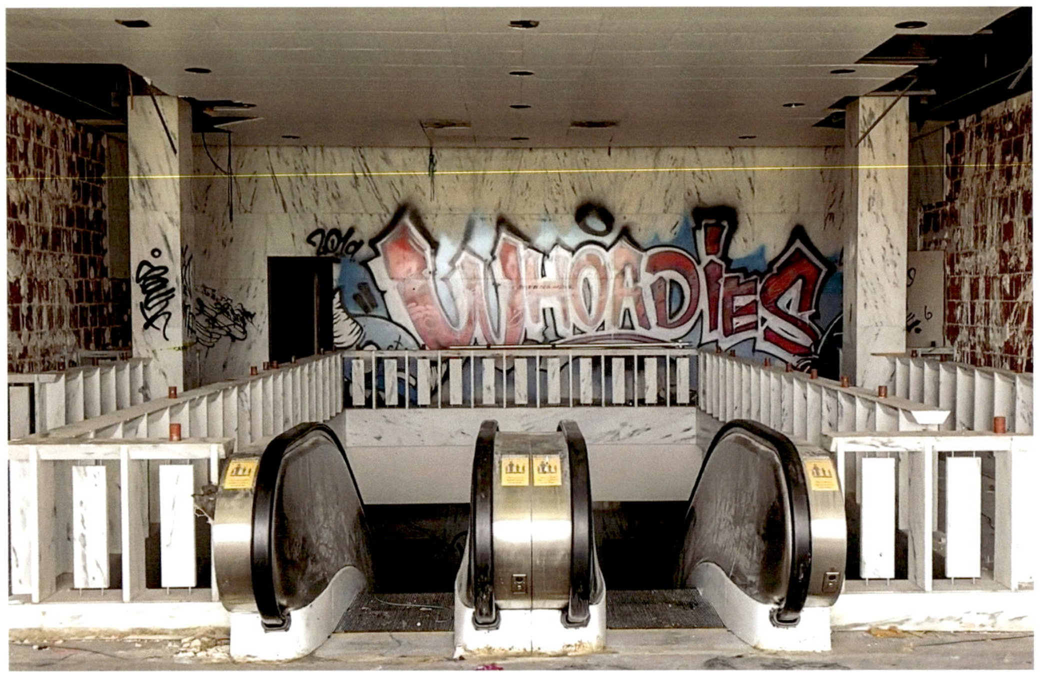

The uppermost level of the main lobby, the escalators now only lead to a desolate space.

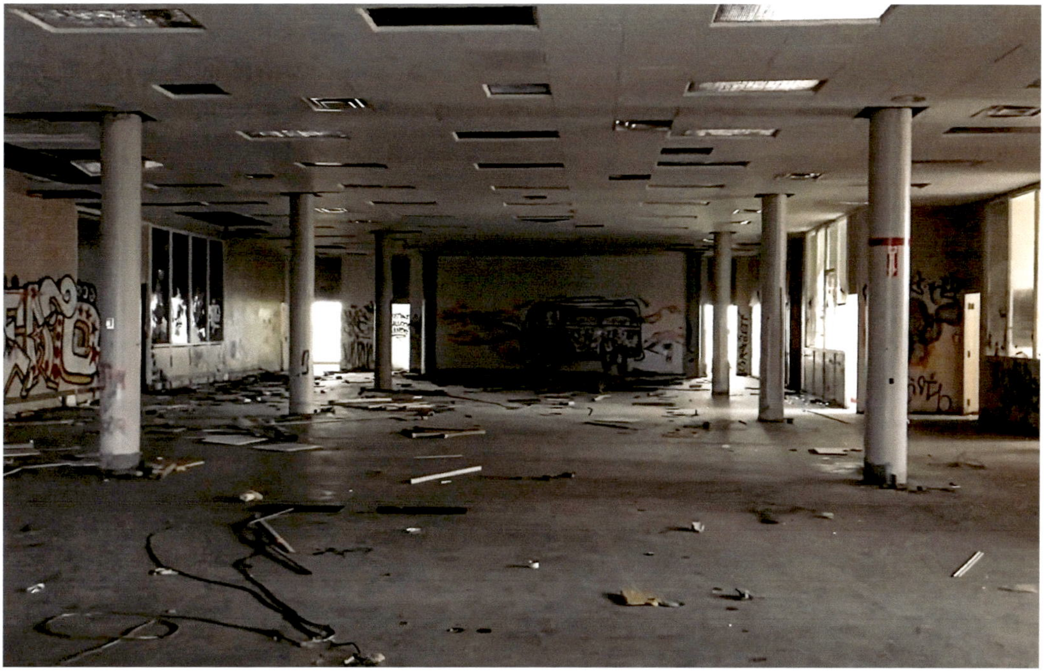

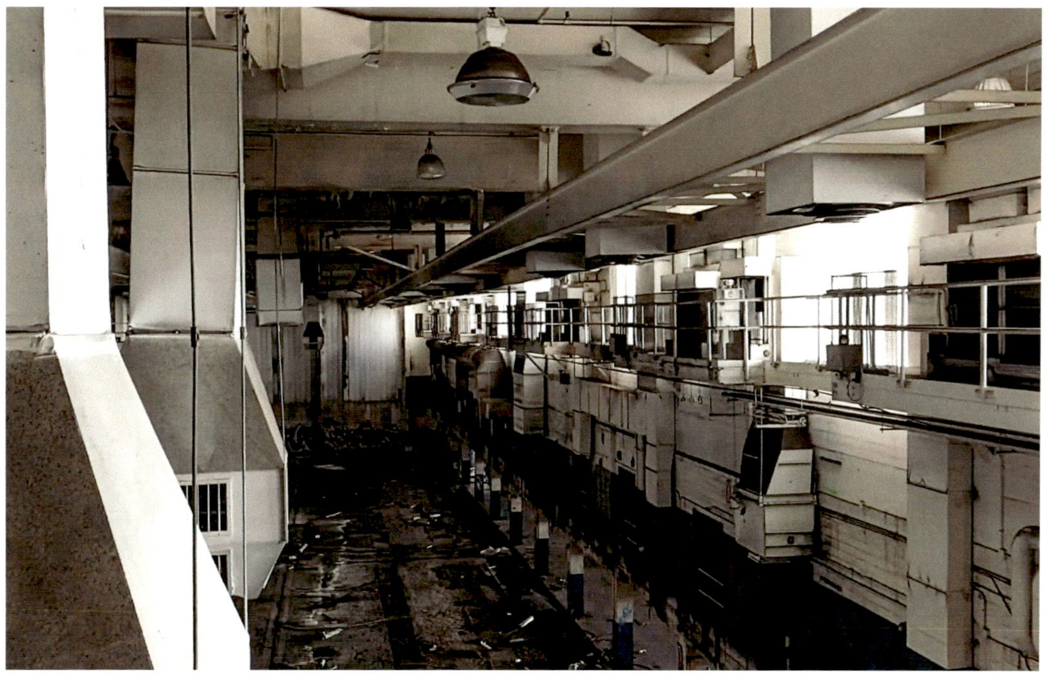

The vast expanse of the former newsroom now stripped bare. This space once buzzed with the energy of breaking news and deadlines but now stands silent, littered with debris.

The machinery that churned out the daily news has long been removed, leaving only traces of the past where countless newspapers were printed.

12

TOURO-SHAKSPEARE NURSING HOME

Echoes of Compassion Amid Decay

Tucked away in the Algiers neighborhood sits the old Touro-Shakspeare Nursing Home. According to the Preservation Resource Center of New Orleans, it was built in 1933 to provide long-term care for the elderly and those with chronic health conditions. The nursing home was named in part to honor the Touro family, known for their contributions to healthcare in the region. The facility offered a range of services designed to meet the needs of its residents, including skilled nursing care, rehabilitation, and supportive services.

Prior to this location, the Touro Almshouse was built in 1862, and was named after Judah Touro who was a local philanthropist. It was located in the Bywater neighborhood and was a grand castle-like structure. Just a few years after it was built, a fire would destroy the first building. So a new location was chosen and the former mayor, Joseph Shakspeare, used gambling tax money to construct a new building in the Uptown area of New Orleans.

In 1933, due to the major growth happening in the area, the home was moved to its final location in Algiers. The new home had room for 200 residents and featured a beautiful chapel with a domed ceiling in the center of the two wings of the building.

As with the majority of the deserted places mentioned in this book, the devastating impact of Hurricane Katrina in 2005 profoundly affected the nursing home. As the storm surged through New Orleans, the nursing home faced severe challenges, including flooding, power outages, and extensive damage to the building's infrastructure.

The hurricane's floodwaters overwhelmed the facility, causing significant damage. The crisis led to an urgent evacuation, with many residents being relocated to temporary shelters and other care facilities. The disaster exposed vulnerabilities in the facility's preparedness and highlighted the broader challenges faced by healthcare institutions in the face of natural calamities.

Despite efforts to restore the nursing home to its former state, the challenges of recovery proved insurmountable. The damage and the evolving needs of the community led to the decision to close the facility permanently. The nursing home was officially shuttered in the years following the hurricane, marking the end of its long-standing role in the New Orleans healthcare system.

After its closure, the building fell into disrepair and became a vacant site. The facility fell to the effects of neglect and deterioration. Over time, the building's condition worsened, with environmental factors contributing to its decline.

This was my very first exploration of a deserted place. On my first visit, I went with a couple of old friends, and a few years later, I returned twice more with the Krewe du Exploration. Each time we visited, we encountered other people. Some were living there, and others (like us) were documenting the building's beauty.

The highlight of this site was undoubtedly the chapel. During my first visit, it was still in relatively good condition, with its charm and character intact. By the time of my second visit, the chapel had deteriorated significantly, though it remained breathtaking in its own way.

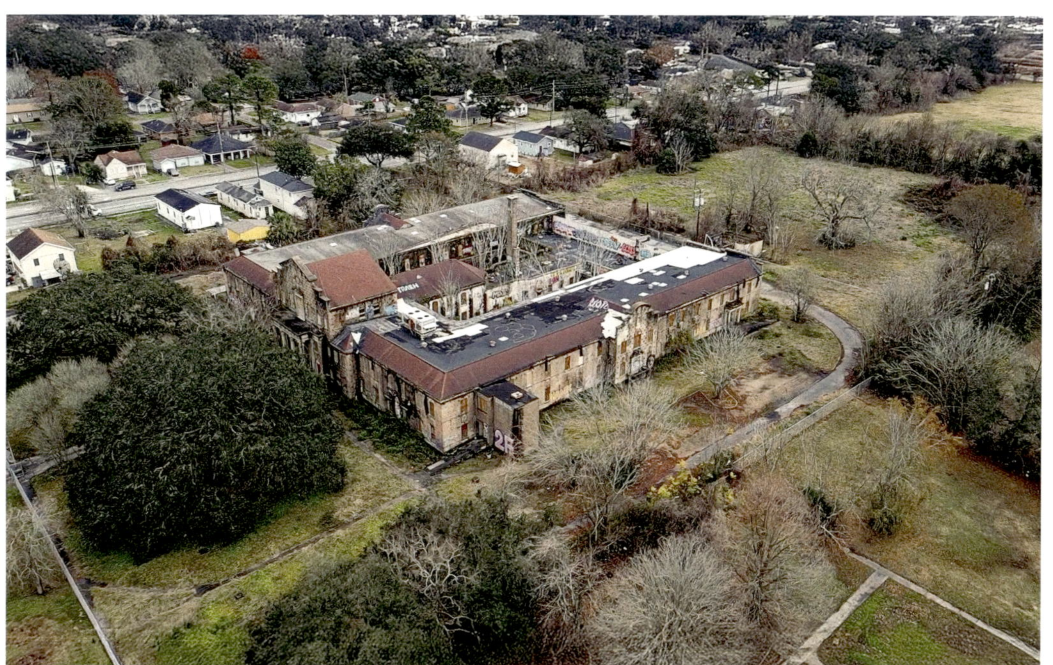

The Touro-Shakspeare Nursing Home, which opened its doors in 1933, was originally established to care for the elderly in New Orleans. By the early 2000s, the facility faced challenges from rising maintenance costs, stricter healthcare regulations, and declining funding. These factors along with the devastation from Hurricane Katrina led to its closure in 2005.

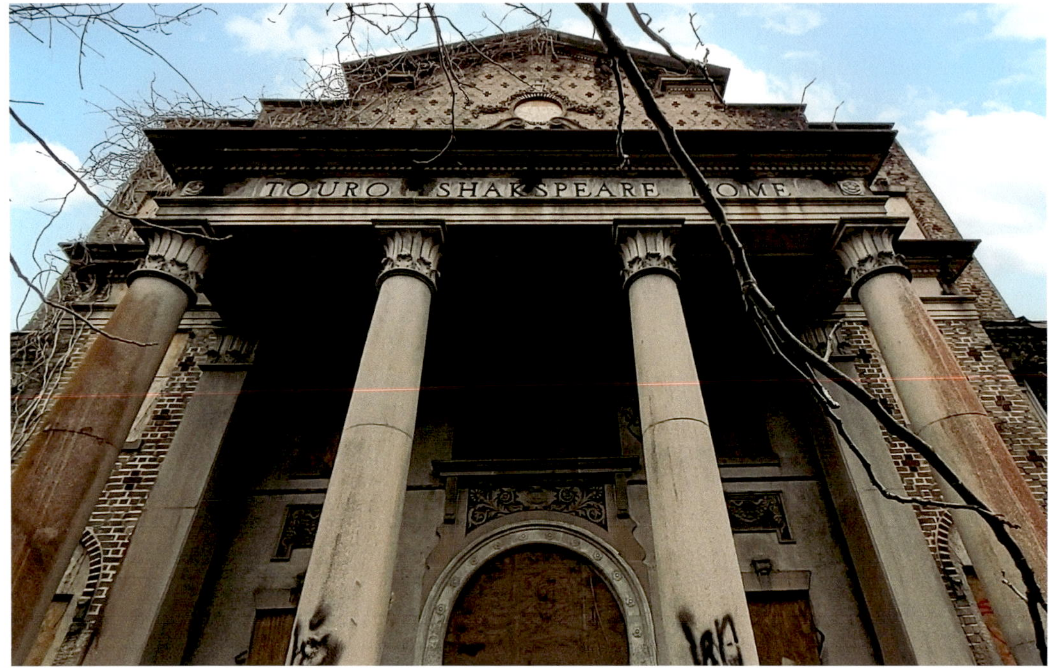

The imposing columns still exude a sense of grandeur despite years of neglect. The weathered facade and once-inviting entryway now loom as haunting relics, with the boarded windows hiding what lies within.

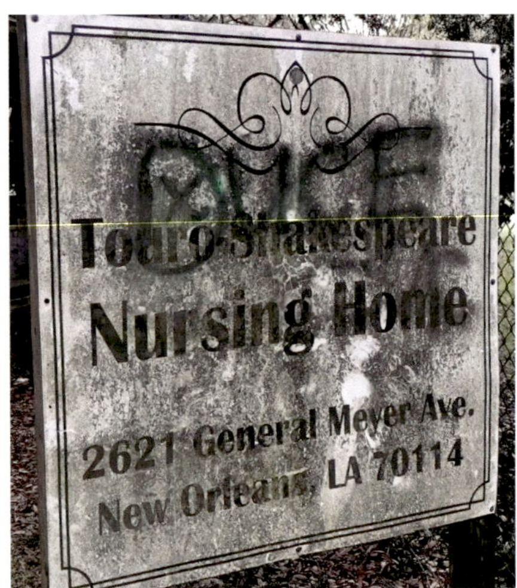

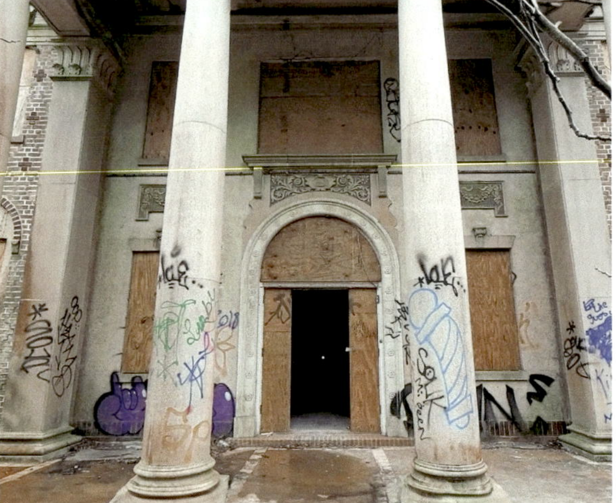

Above left: The weathered sign still stands marking the entrance to what was once a respected care facility. Today, the sign bears the marks of time and vandalism, symbolizing the fate of the old nursing home beyond it.

Above right: The stark contrast between the building's elegant architectural details and its current state speaks to years of neglect and desertion.

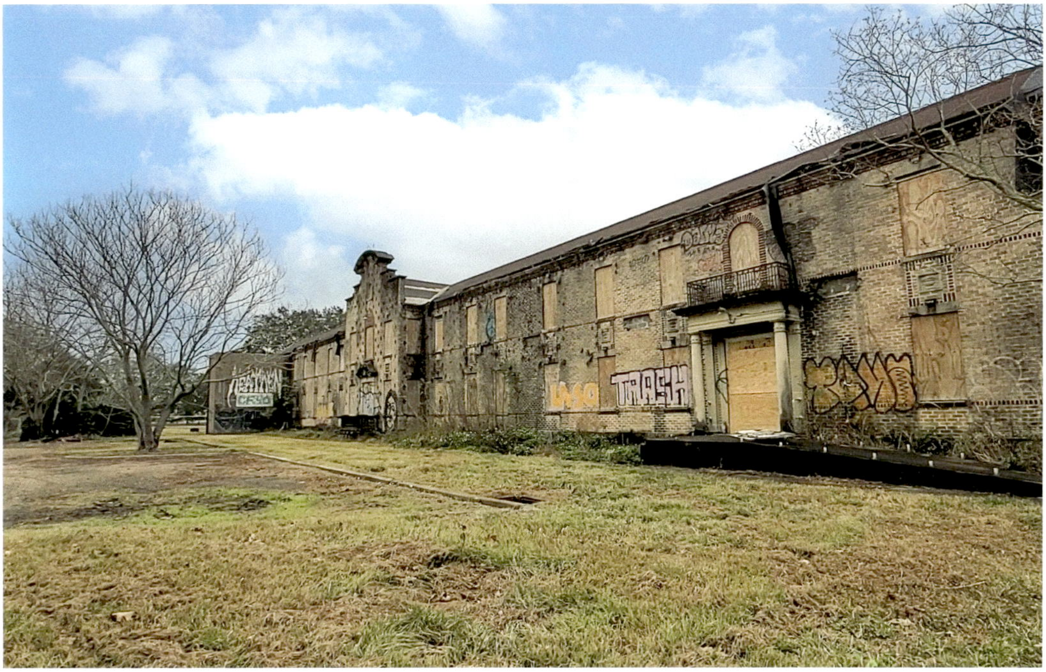

Boarded windows and broken balconies hint at decades of vacancy. The surrounding grounds are desolate, adding to the air of abandonment that permeates the site. The structure, though battered by time, still commands attention with its imposing presence.

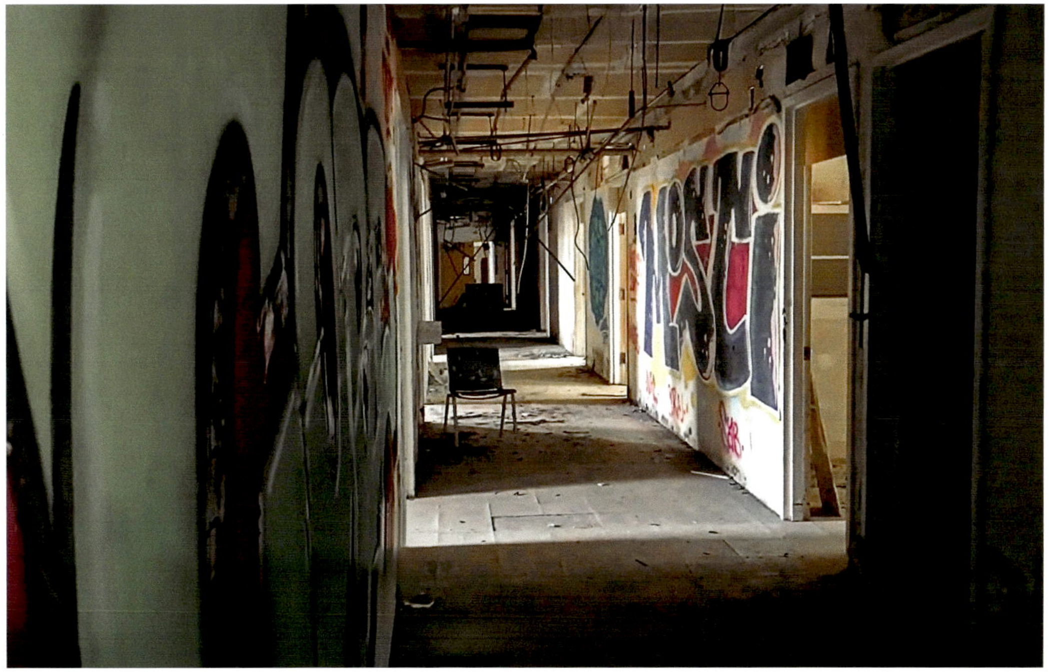

A lonely chair sits in one of the corridors as a reminder of its past use. As sunlight filters through broken doorways, it casts eerie shadows that dance across the debris-strewn floor, hinting at the stories left behind in these forgotten walls.

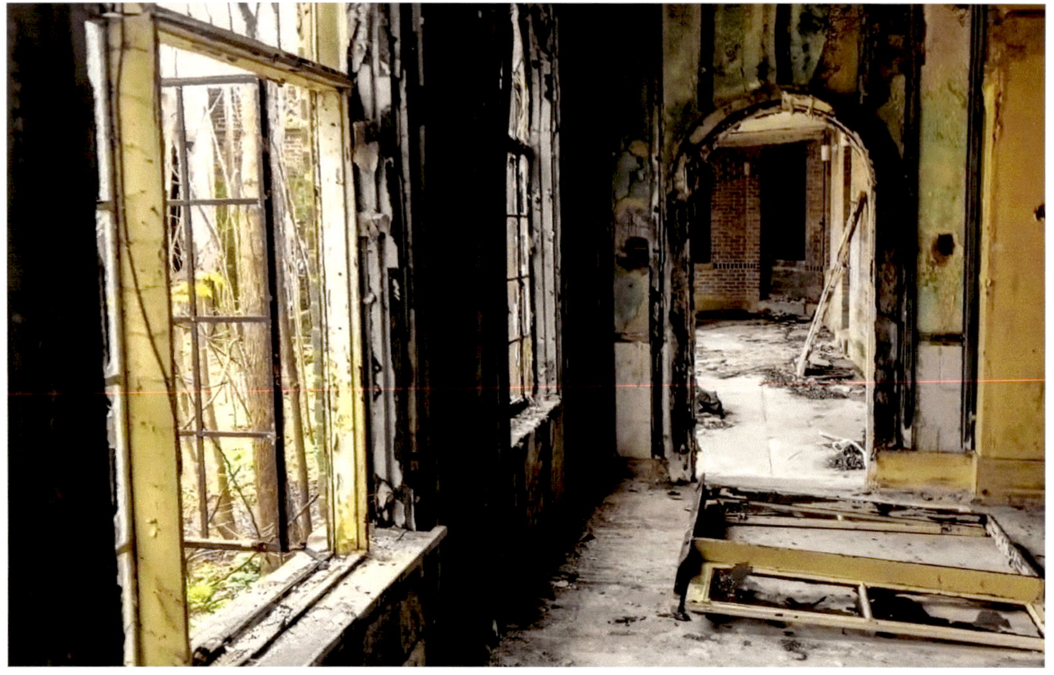

The peeling paint, broken frames, and arched doorways hint at the building's former elegance. Now, nature creeps in through the cracked glass, reclaiming what has been left behind.

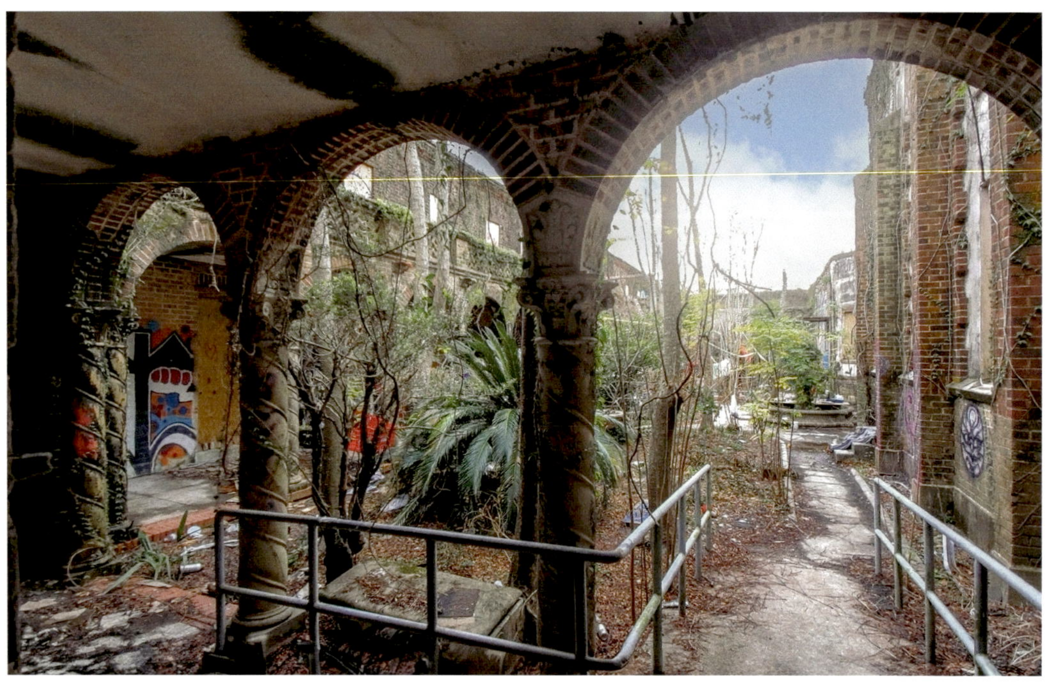

Lush vegetation has taken over the courtyards of the old building, blending with the ornate brick arches.

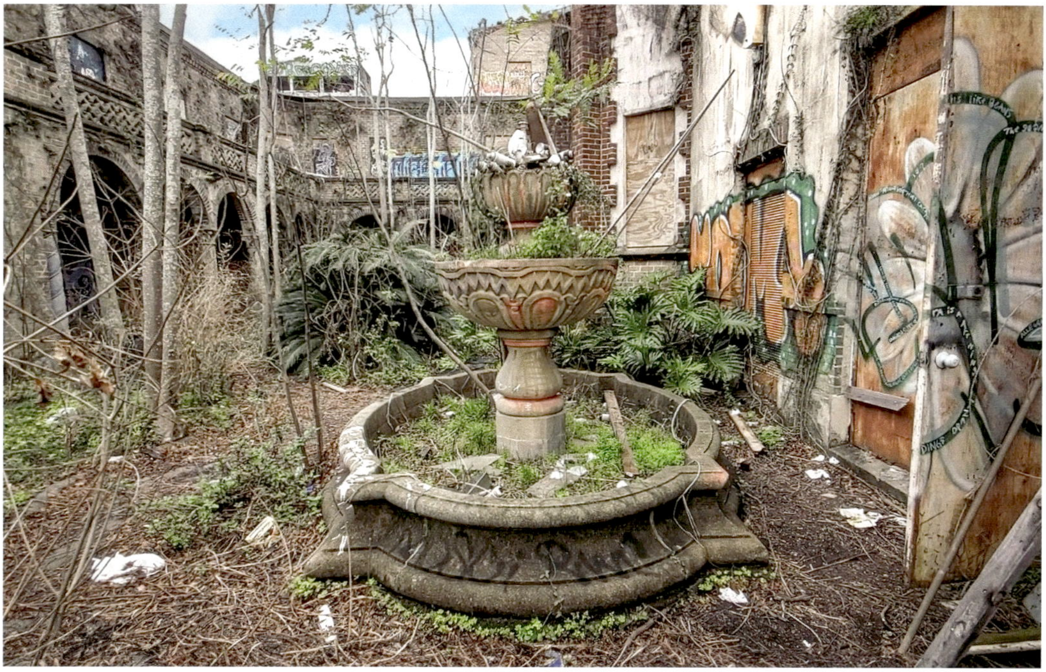

A forgotten fountain sits in one of the two courtyards. Once a centerpiece of tranquility, the intricate stonework is slowly being swallowed by nature.

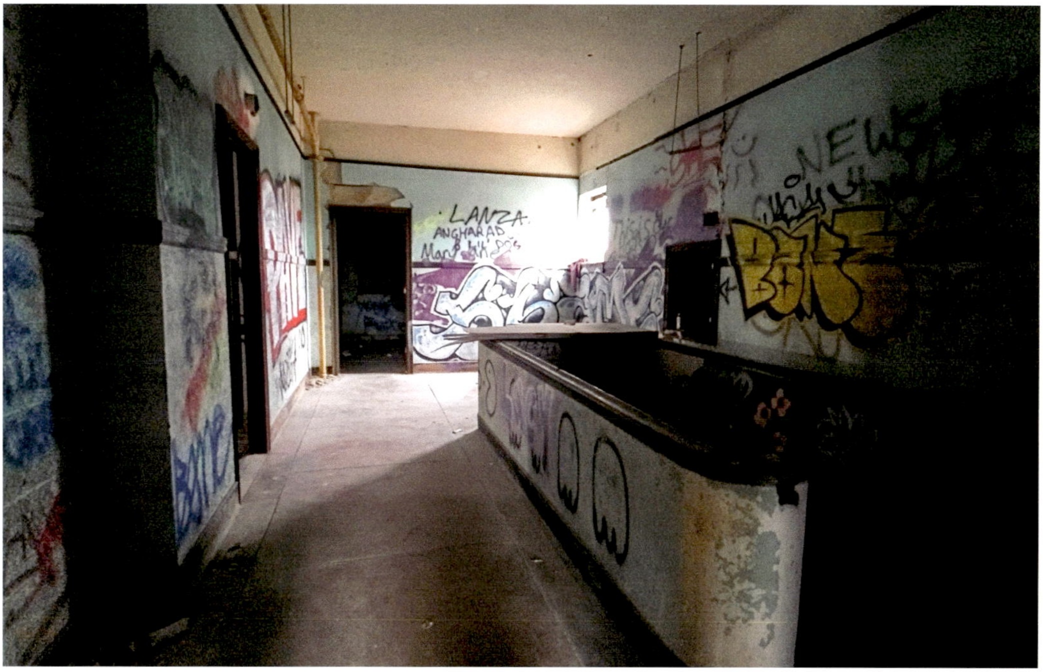

The faded paint and dim light filtering through broken windows create an atmosphere where the past feels almost palpable. Vandalism and decay have taken over, turning the stairwell into an art-filled, yet eerie relic of a bygone era.

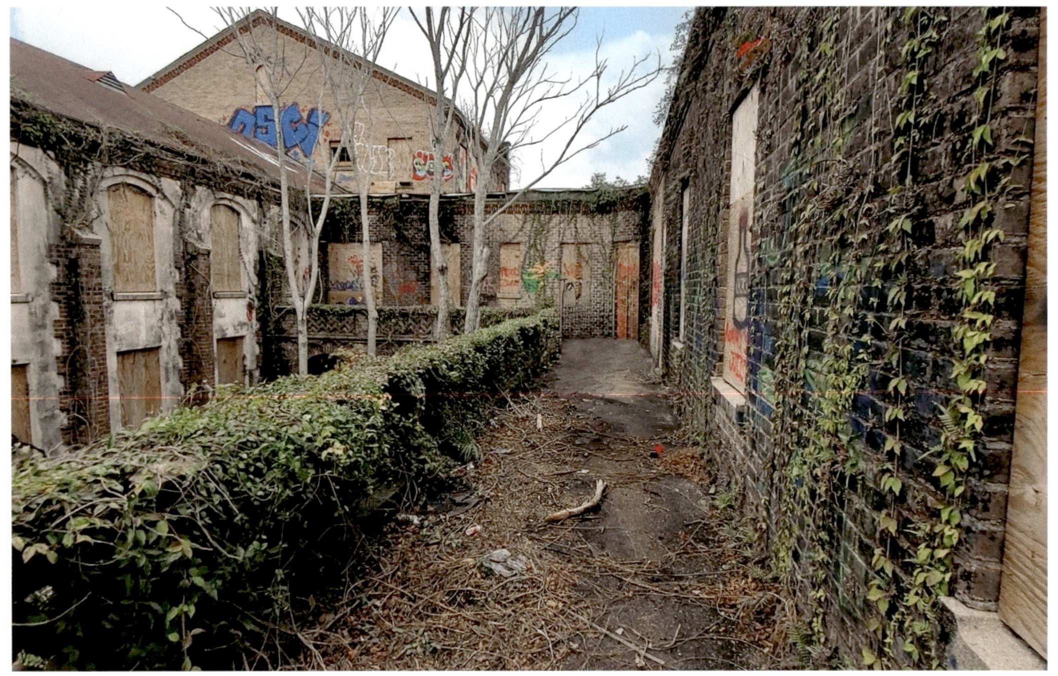

The overgrown balcony offers a view of what was once a serene courtyard below. Now, creeping ivy and graffiti-covered walls dominate the scene.

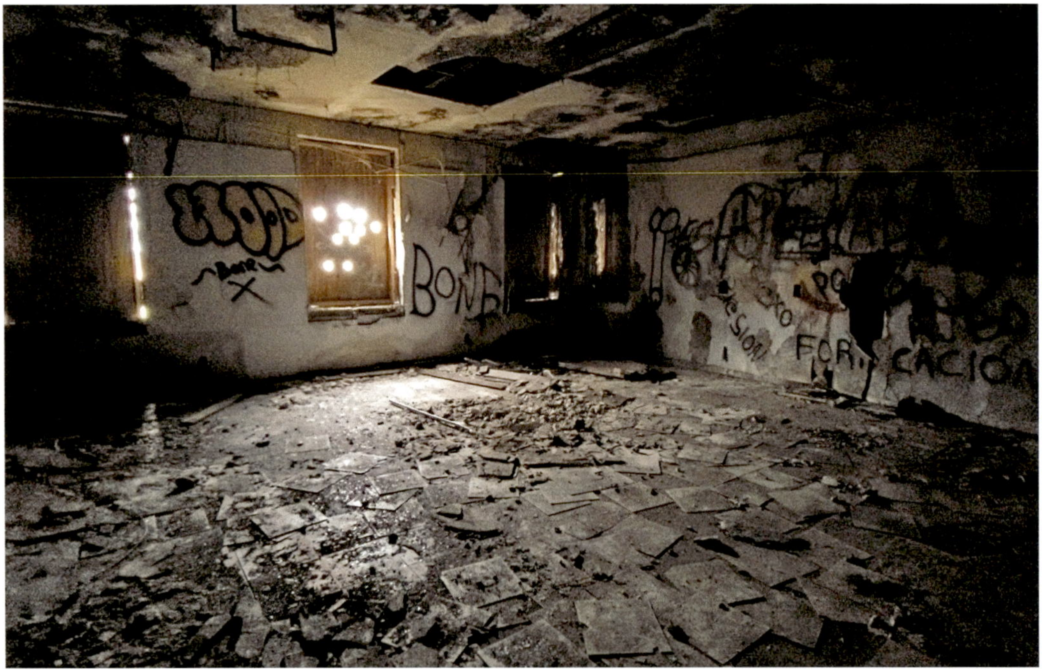

Light seeps through holes in a boarded-up window. The room now lies in ruins, with broken tiles and scattered debris covering the ground.

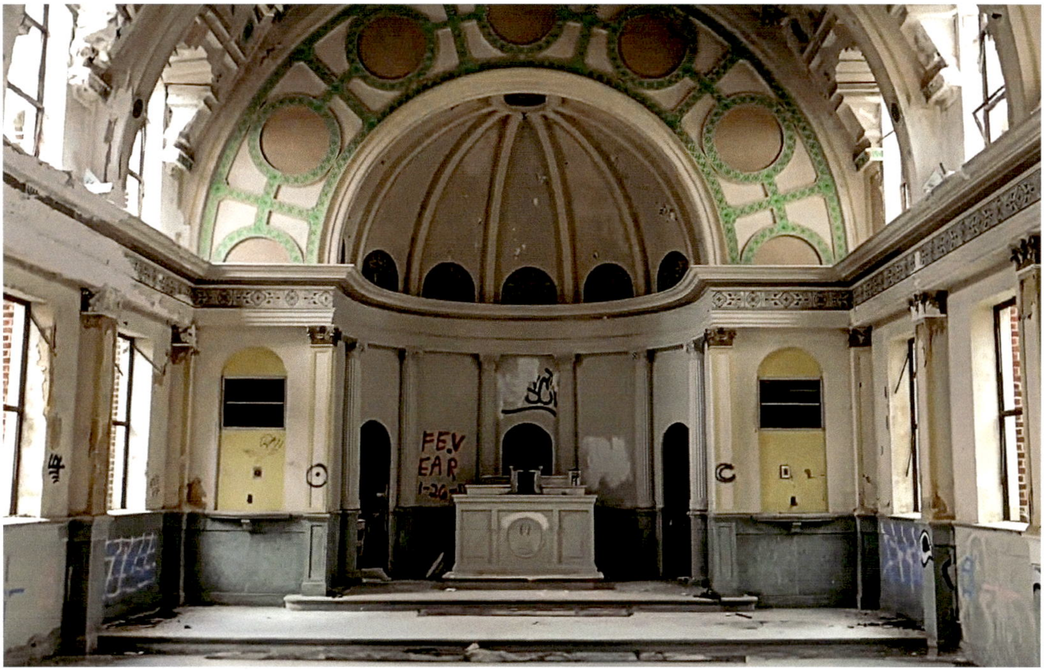

The once-grand chapel now stands in silence, its ornate arches and domed ceiling still showcasing hints of the past. The faded green and cream detailing adds a splash of color amid the crumbling plaster and graffiti-tagged walls.

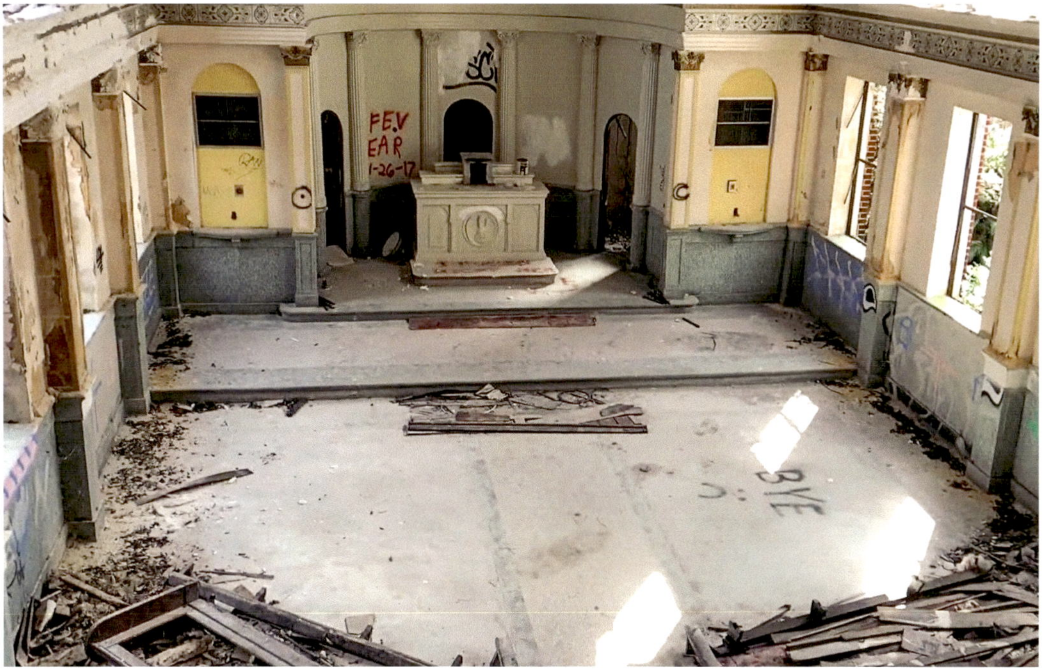

From the balcony above, you can see some of the chapel's former wooden pews. They have been reduced to rubble after years of neglect but the altar still stands.

CONCLUSION

Exploring deserted places has been one of the most rewarding and fascinating pursuits of my life. The thrill of venturing into forgotten corners of the world, capturing their haunting beauty through photography, and piecing together their histories is something I will never grow tired of. Every site tells a story sometimes of triumph and progress, other times of tragedy and neglect. Documenting these places allows me to preserve a small piece of their narrative, to give voice to spaces that would otherwise be lost to time.

That said, I cannot stress enough how dangerous this activity can be. The risks are very real. Crumbling floors, hidden hazards, sharp rusted objects, and even harmful substances left behind are all real risks that can be encountered. Without the proper precautions, the consequences can be severe. In addition, without permission, entering these places is considered trespassing and is against the law. For anyone considering urban exploration, I urge you to think carefully, plan thoroughly, and respect the laws and risks involved.

What keeps me coming back to these places is not just adventure, it is the layers of history waiting to be uncovered. Whether it is finding amazing graffiti art tucked away in an old building or seeing items that have not been touched in decades, or learning the good and bad of a site's past, each experience adds depth to my understanding of the world around me. At the same time, there are sobering moments, like discovering syringes and needles used for hard drugs, reminders of the struggles some people face.

Urban exploration is not just about the places themselves, it is about the emotions they evoke and the stories they tell. Through this book, I hope to have conveyed the wonder, the sadness, and the respect I feel for these sites. While I strongly encourage curiosity about the world's forgotten spaces, I urge everyone to approach with caution, respect, and responsibility. These places have much to teach us, but they demand careful and thoughtful exploration.